Math Expressions

Homework and Remembering • Volume 1

Developed by
The Children's Math Worlds Research Project

PROJECT DIRECTOR AND AUTHOR
Dr. Karen C. Fuson

This material is based upon work supported by the
National Science Foundation
under Grant Numbers
ESI-9816320, REC-9806020, and RED-935373.

Any opinions, findings, and conclusions, or recommendations expressed in this material
are those of the author and do not necessarily reflect the views of the National Science Foundation.

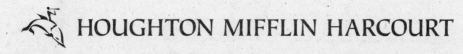
HOUGHTON MIFFLIN HARCOURT

Teacher Reviewers

Kindergarten
Patricia Stroh Sugiyama
Wilmette, Illinois

Barbara Wahle
Evanston, Illinois

Grade 1
Sandra Budson
Newton, Massachusetts

Janet Pecci
Chicago, Illinois

Megan Rees
Chicago, Illinois

Grade 2
Molly Dunn
Danvers, Massachusetts

Agnes Lesnick
Hillside, Illinois

Rita Soto
Chicago, Illinois

Grade 3
Jane Curran
Honesdale, Pennsylvania

Sandra Tucker
Chicago, Illinois

Grade 4
Sara Stoneberg Llibre
Chicago, Illinois

Sheri Roedel
Chicago, Illinois

Grade 5
Todd Atler
Chicago, Illinois

Leah Barry
Norfolk, Massachusetts

Credits

Cover art: © Kerstin Layer/Age Fotostock

Ilustrative art: Robin Boyer/Deborah Wolfe, LTD; Geoff Smith
Technical art: Nesbitt Graphics, Inc.
Photos: Nesbitt Graphics, Inc.

Printed in the U.S.A.

ISBN: 978-0-547-47941-5

1 2 3 4 5 6 7 8 9 10 1689 19 18 17 16 15 14 13 12 11 10

4500229321   X B C D E

Homework

Write an equation for each situation. Then solve the problem.

Show your work.

1. Carol wrote 9 poems in her journal. Then, she wrote 7 more poems. How many poems did Carol write in her journal in all?

   _____

2. Jaipal had 14 pages left to read of his book. So far, he read 8 pages. How many pages does Jaipal have left to read?

   _____

3. Kele walked 6 blocks to the library. Then, he walked 6 blocks home. How many blocks did Kele walk in total?

   _____

4. Julieta had 18 photos in all. She took 9 of these photos and her friend took the others. How many photos did her friend take?

   _____

5. Inez worked 7 hours on Monday. Then, she worked 5 hours on Tuesday. How many hours did Inez work altogether?

   _____

6. Dwight has 13 problems for math homework. He has finished 7 of the problems. How many more problems does Dwight have to finish?

   _____

Remembering

Use the information in the bar graph to answer the questions.

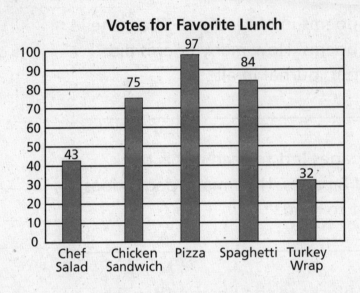

Votes for Favorite Lunch

1. How many more votes did the chicken sandwich receive than the turkey wrap?

_____

2. How many votes did the chef salad and the spaghetti receive in all?

_____

3. How many fewer votes did the spaghetti receive than the pizza?

_____

4. How many more votes are needed so the chicken sandwich would have the same number of votes as the spaghetti?

_____

Add or subtract.

5. $\begin{array}{r} 746 \\ -\ 538 \\ \hline \end{array}$

6. $\begin{array}{r} 873 \\ -\ 492 \\ \hline \end{array}$

7. $\begin{array}{r} 628 \\ +\ 173 \\ \hline \end{array}$

8. $\begin{array}{r} \$4.57 \\ +\$3.62 \\ \hline \end{array}$

Continue the number pattern. Write the rule.

9. 22, 28, 34, _____, _____, _____, _____, _____   Rule: _____

Basic Additions and Subtractions

Name _____   Date _____

Homework

Write the number for each drawing.

1.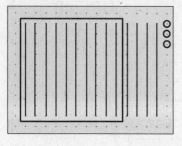

_____

2.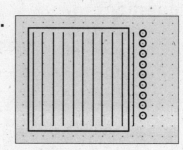

_____

3.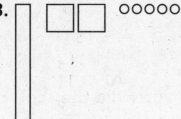

_____

4.

_____

Make a place value drawing for each number.

5. 431

6. 1,214

Write the number for the words.

7. one thousand sixty

_____

8. four thousand, three hundred

_____

9. ninety-seven

_____

10. four hundred fifty-four

_____

Remembering

Add or subtract.

J. 9 + 4	**I.** 8 + 7	**C.** 6 + 5	**U.** 9 + 8

R. 5 + 6	**E.** 8 + 3	**M.** 8 + 8	**L.** 7 + 6

K. 10 − 6	**N.** 7 − 4	**S.** 3 − 2	**A.** 11 − 6

T. 8 − 6	**F.** 12 − 4	**B.** 5 − 1	**H.** 10 − 3

Use the letters and the answers above to help you find the secret code.

___ ___ ___ ___   ___ ___   ___ ___ ___
16   5   2   7   15   1   8   17   3

Name _____ **Date** _____

Homework

Write the money value for each place value drawing.

1.

_____

2.

_____

3.

_____

4.

_____

Make a place value drawing to represent each money amount.

5. $1.63

6. $5.15

Write the number.

7. 7 hundreds + 6 tens + 5 ones _____

8. 4 hundreds + 3 ones _____

9. 2 hundreds + 7 tens _____

10. 2 thousands + 9 tens + 8 ones _____

Build Numbers and Represent Money Amounts **5**

Remembering

Add.

1.   8
  + 4
  _____

2.   9
  + 3
  _____

3.   5
  + 5
  _____

4.   4
  + 7
  _____

5.   6
  + 7
  _____

6.   7
  + 3
  _____

7.   9
  + 7
  _____

8.   8
  + 8
  _____

Subtract.

9.   13
  − 9
  _____

10.   17
  − 8
  _____

11.   16
  − 6
  _____

12.   11
  − 3
  _____

13.   12
  − 4
  _____

14.   16
  − 7
  _____

15.   17
  − 9
  _____

16.   14
  − 6
  _____

Solve each problem. Label your answer.

17. On Tuesday, 3 students gave their reports in the morning. Then, 4 students gave their reports in the afternoon. How many students gave their reports on Tuesday?

Show your work.

_____

18. Rick has 12 sheets of poster board. He uses 4 sheets for his project on Saturn. How many sheets of poster board does he have left?

_____

Build Numbers and Represent Money Amounts

Name _____ Date _____

Homework

Use place value drawings to help you solve each problem. Label your answers.

> At Kyle's birthday party, he gave each of his 8 friends a bag. Each bag had 10 party favors.

1. How many favors did Kyle give out altogether?

_____

> A farmer had 612 tomatoes. He put them in baskets of 100.

2. How many baskets did he fill completely?

_____

3. How many tomatoes were left over?

_____

> At the library, Eric is placing 112 books on shelves. Each shelf holds 10 books.

4. How many shelves can Eric fill completely?

_____

5. How many books will be left over?

_____

Write the number for the words.

6. one hundred sixty-seven _____   **7.** eighty-two _____

8. one hundred twenty _____   **9.** fifteen _____

10. four thousand one hundred six _____

11. one thousand ninety-nine _____

Remembering

Add or subtract.

1. $\begin{array}{r} 9 \\ +\,8 \\ \hline \end{array}$
2. $\begin{array}{r} 7 \\ +\,6 \\ \hline \end{array}$
3. $\begin{array}{r} 13 \\ -\,9 \\ \hline \end{array}$
4. $\begin{array}{r} 17 \\ -\,8 \\ \hline \end{array}$
5. $\begin{array}{r} 16 \\ -\,7 \\ \hline \end{array}$

6. $\begin{array}{r} 5 \\ +\,6 \\ \hline \end{array}$
7. $\begin{array}{r} 8 \\ +\,7 \\ \hline \end{array}$
8. $\begin{array}{r} 4 \\ +\,9 \\ \hline \end{array}$
9. $\begin{array}{r} 14 \\ -\,6 \\ \hline \end{array}$
10. $\begin{array}{r} 12 \\ -\,4 \\ \hline \end{array}$

11. $\begin{array}{r} 8 \\ +\,6 \\ \hline \end{array}$
12. $\begin{array}{r} 5 \\ +\,7 \\ \hline \end{array}$
13. $\begin{array}{r} 18 \\ -\,9 \\ \hline \end{array}$
14. $\begin{array}{r} 15 \\ -\,9 \\ \hline \end{array}$
15. $\begin{array}{r} 11 \\ -\,4 \\ \hline \end{array}$

16. $\begin{array}{r} 3 \\ +\,7 \\ \hline \end{array}$
17. $\begin{array}{r} 7 \\ +\,7 \\ \hline \end{array}$
18. $\begin{array}{r} 6 \\ +\,2 \\ \hline \end{array}$
19. $\begin{array}{r} 11 \\ -\,5 \\ \hline \end{array}$
20. $\begin{array}{r} 17 \\ -\,9 \\ \hline \end{array}$

Complete.

21. $7 + 9 = $ _____

$70 + 90 = $ _____

$700 + 900 = $ _____

22. $3 + 9 = $ _____

$30 + 90 = $ _____

$300 + 900 = $ _____

23. $6 + 6 = $ _____

$60 + 60 = $ _____

$600 + 600 = $ _____

24. $8 + 5 = $ _____

$80 + 50 = $ _____

$800 + 500 = $ _____

25. $7 + 4 = $ _____

$70 + 40 = $ _____

$700 + 400 = $ _____

26. $9 + 6 = $ _____

$90 + 60 = $ _____

$900 + 600 = $ _____

Name _____   **Date** _____

Homework

Unscramble the place values and write the number.

1. 5 hundreds + 0 ones + 8 tens

_____

2. 2 ones + 1 ten + 7 hundreds

_____

3. 9 hundreds + 0 tens + 8 ones

_____

4. 7 tens + 7 hundreds + 3 ones

_____

5. 3 tens + 1 one + 2 hundreds

_____

6. 3 ones + 2 hundreds + 9 tens

_____

Solve each problem. Label your answer.

Ms. Chang gave a box of 10 colored pencils to each of her 17 students.

7. How many pencils did Ms. Chang give out?

_____

The Finicky Bakery puts exactly 100 raisins in each carrot cake they bake. They have 233 raisins.

8. How many carrot cakes can they make?

_____

9. How many raisins will be left over?

_____

Dora won 146 prize tickets at the town fair. She needs 10 tickets to get a small toy.

10. How many toys can she get with her tickets?

_____

11. How many tickets will she have left?

_____

Remembering

Make a place value drawing for each number.

1. 382

2. 567

3. 1,430

4. 1,215

Write the number for each drawing.

5. ▢ ||| ∘∘∘∘∘
∘

_____

6.

_____

_____

8. ▯ ▢ ||| ∘

_____

**Complete to show how you can find the sum by
making a ten, hundred, or thousand.**

9. $8 + 5 =$

　$\boxed{8 + 2}$ + _____

　$\boxed{10}$ + _____

　_____

10. $80 + 50 =$

　$\boxed{80 + 20}$ + _____

　$\boxed{100}$ + _____

　_____

11. $800 + 500 =$

　$\boxed{800 + 200}$ + _____

　$\boxed{1,000}$ + _____

　_____

Practice with Place Value

Name _____   Date _____

Homework

Solve using a numerical method and a proof drawing.

1. Nadia had 392 stickers. She bought 647 more. How many stickers does she have now?

   _____

2. South Elementary School has 937 students. North Elementary School has 786 students. How many students do the schools have altogether?

   _____

3. 329 + 755 = _____

4. 839 + 492 _____

5. 612 + 216 = _____

6. 1,231 + 397 = _____

Unscramble the place values and write the number.

7. 4 hundreds + 2 tens + 6 thousands + 5 ones _____

8. 7 ones + 3 hundreds + 8 thousands _____

9. 3 tens + 5 thousands + 9 hundreds _____

Name _____ **Date** _____

Remembering

Subtract.

1. $13 - 8 =$ _____   2. $11 - 7 =$ _____   3. $15 - 6 =$ _____

   $130 - 80 =$ _____ $110 - 70 =$ _____ $150 - 60 =$ _____

   $1,300 - 800 =$ _____ $1,100 - 700 =$ _____ $1,500 - 600 =$ _____

Solve each problem. Draw a place value drawing if you need to. Label your answers.

4. At the end-of-year party, 10 students played   *Show your work.*
   Pin the Tail on the Donkey. Each student had
   5 turns to try to pin the tail on the donkey.
   How many turns were taken in all?

   _____

5. Loni had 8 blank CDs. She recorded 10 songs
   on each CD. What was the total number of
   songs Loni recorded?

   _____

6. Ali has 128 photos of her pets and 255 photos
   of her family. How many photos does Ali have
   altogether?

   _____

7. James has 112 baseball cards. Each page of his
   scrapbook holds 10 cards. How many pages can
   he fill? How many cards will be left over?

   _____

Explore Multi-Digit Addition

Homework

Solve using a numerical method and a proof drawing.

1. Delia guessed that there were 1,534 beans in a jar. When the contest ended, the beans were counted. There were 752 more beans than Delia guessed. How many beans were in the jar?

_____

2. Sal's Sandwich Shop sold 1,324 sandwiches last week. This week they sold 679 more sandwiches than they sold last week. How many sandwiches did the shop sell this week?

_____

3. An on-line music store sold 1,038 CDs on Monday and 1,025 CDs on Tuesday. How many CDs did the store sell on those two days?

_____

Write each addition vertically. Line up the places correctly and add. Make a proof drawing to show your answer is correct.

4. 657 + 69 = _____ | 5. 459 + 1,265 = _____ | 6. 1,056 + 99 = _____

Name _____ **Date** _____

Remembering

Solve. Label your answers.

1. Mr. Liam bought 8 boxes of tissues. There are 100 tissues in each box. How many tissues did he buy in all?

   _____

Bryan has 387 crayons. He can fit 100 crayons in each box.

2. How many boxes can he fill?

   _____

3. How many crayons will be left over?

   _____

Add or subtract.

4. 5 + 6 = _____   5. 7 + 6 = _____   6. 9 + 7 = _____

7. 8 + 4 = _____   8. 16 − 7 = _____   9. 15 − 9 = _____

10. 14 − 6 = _____   11. 11 − 4 = _____   12. 17 − 8 = _____

Complete to show how you can find the sum by making a ten, hundred, or thousand.

13. 9 + 5 =   14. 90 + 50 =   15. 900 + 500 =

    [9 + 1] + _____   [90 + 10] + _____   [900 + 100] + _____

    [10] + _____   [100] + _____   [1,000] + _____

    _____   _____   _____

Discuss Addition Methods

Homework

Use the grocery store items on Student Activity Book page 21 to answer these questions.

1. Stacey bought a loaf of bread and some lettuce. How much did her items cost? _____

2. Jing bought 2 watermelons to serve at the school celebration. How much did the watermelons cost? _____

3. Lani bought a bunch of bananas and some milk. How much did she spend? _____

4. **Challenge** Willie bought cheese, a head of lettuce, a loaf of bread, and a tomato. How much did he spend? _____

Write each addition vertically. Then add. Make a proof drawing if you need to.

5. 827 + 354   6. 1,771 + 209   7. 479 + 1,253

   _____   _____   _____

Name _____ Date _____

Remembering

Solve. Label your answers. Make a place value drawing if you need to.

Show your work.

1. Jessica bought 3 boxes of envelopes. Each box contained 100 envelopes. How many envelopes did she buy in all?

_____

2. Leo has 421 prize tickets. He can get 1 prize for every 100 tickets. How many prizes can Leo get? How many tickets will he have left over?

_____

3. Charity has 4 boxes of paper clips. Each box has 100 paper clips. How many more boxes does Charity need in order to have 500 paper clips?

_____

4. Neil buys 5 bags of marbles. Each bag has 10 marbles. He gives 10 marbles to Sam. How many marbles does Neil have now?

_____

Use mental math to add or subtract.

5. $40 + 70 =$ _____   **6.** $140 - 80 =$ _____   **7.** $130 - 70 =$ _____

Find each sum.

8. $3 + 8 + 5 =$ _____   **9.** $6 + 6 + 3 =$ _____   **10.** $3 + 9 + 7 =$ _____

11. $7 + 6 + 4 =$ _____   **12.** $8 + 8 + 1 =$ _____   **13.** $4 + 5 + 1 =$ _____

Addition with Dollars and Cents

Homework

Write each addition vertically. Decide which new groups you will make. Then, add to see if you were correct.

1. 256 + 1,273 _____

A new ten? _____

A new hundred? _____

A new thousand? _____

2. 784 + 1,041 _____

A new ten? _____

A new hundred? _____

A new thousand? _____

3. 184 + 924 _____

A new ten? _____

A new hundred? _____

A new thousand? _____

Add.

4.   690
      + 421
      _____

5.   1,512
      + 355
      _____

6.   1,629
      +   78
      _____

7. $2.39
      + 0.74
      _____

8. $1.98
      + 2.99
      _____

9. $11.99
      + 2.27
      _____

Remembering

Make a place value drawing for each number.

1. 1,052

2. 907

3. 126

4. 1,203

Add.

5. 165
    + 481

6. 578
    + 329

7. 259
    + 672

8. 457
    + 175

9. Write a word problem for one of the addition
exercises above.

_____

_____

_____

Use mental math to add or subtract.

10. $500 + 600 =$ _____

11. $1,200 - 800 =$ _____

12. $900 + 900 =$ _____

13. $1,500 - 700 =$ _____

14. $9 + 11 + 2 =$ _____

15. $3 + 5 + 7 =$ _____

16. $7 + 7 + 7 =$ _____

17. $16 + 4 + 5 =$ _____

18. $2 + 8 + 7 =$ _____

The Grouping Concept in Addition

Homework

Use the menu from Carmen's Cafe on Student Book page 25 to solve each problem.

1. Randy ordered a peanut butter and jelly sandwich and cinnamon apple rings. How much did he spend? _____

2. Jamie and her dad went to lunch. He ordered the chili and cornbread. She ordered the black-eyed peas and rice. What was their bill? _____

3. Rafael ordered the ham and bean delight and a mango shake. What was the total cost?

   _____

4. Teri ordered raspberry ice cream and a melon bowl. How much was her bill? _____

5. Yao gave the saleswoman $3.88 for 2 melon bowls. Is $3.88 the correct amount? If not, explain the error Yao made.

   _____

   _____

   _____

   _____

   _____

Name _____ Date _____

Remembering

Add.

1. 419 + 112 = _____ 2. 236 + 127 = _____ 3. 255 + 566 = _____

4. 727 + 358 = _____ 5. 634 + 818 = _____ 6. 345 + 975 = _____

Unscramble the place values and write the number.

7. 8 tens + 1 thousand _____   8. 5 ones + 6 hundreds _____

9. 1 thousand + 7 hundreds + 3 ones _____

10. 3 hundreds + 4 tens + 1 thousand _____

Solve each problem. Remember to label your answer.

11. Charles and Susan collected cans for recycling.   *Show your work.*
    Charles collected 253 cans. Susan collected 279.
    How many cans did they collect altogether?

    _____

12. Liz has a comic book collection. 255 of her
    books feature Super Girl and the other 648 do
    not. What is the total number of comic books
    in Liz's collection?

    _____

13. At Mr. Beal's fruit stand, there are 157 red
    apples and 68 green apples. What is the total
    number of apples?

    _____

Practice Addition

Homework

**Make a proof drawing and subtract numerically.
Show your ungroupings.**

1. Oksana made 147 bracelets to sell at the art fair.
   By the end of the day Saturday, she had sold 63
   bracelets. How many bracelets did she have left?

   _____

2. Ms. Chao collects buttons. She had 382 buttons,
   but sold 57 of them to other collectors. How
   many buttons does she have left?

   _____

3. On Monday morning, a bookstore had 412
   copies of a popular book. By the end of the day,
   they had sold 153 copies of the book. How
   many copies did they have left?

   _____

**Subtract. Show your ungroupings. Make proof
drawings if you need to.**

4. $\begin{array}{r} 333 \\ -\ 71 \\ \hline \end{array}$

5. $\begin{array}{r} 253 \\ -\ 172 \\ \hline \end{array}$

6. $\begin{array}{r} 435 \\ -\ 89 \\ \hline \end{array}$

7. $\begin{array}{r} 562 \\ -\ 267 \\ \hline \end{array}$

8. $\begin{array}{r} 713 \\ -\ 53 \\ \hline \end{array}$

9. $\begin{array}{r} 825 \\ -\ 716 \\ \hline \end{array}$

Remembering

Write the money value for each drawing.

1.
2.

_____   _____

Unscramble the place values and write the number.

3. 7 tens + 4 hundreds + 2 ones   _____

4. 1 thousand + 8 ones + 3 hundreds   _____

5. 3 hundreds + 5 ones + 1 thousand + 7 tens   _____

6. 4 hundreds + 2 ones + 1 thousand + 5 tens   _____

7. 2 tens + 1 thousand   _____

8. 5 ones + 8 hundreds + 1 thousand   _____

Use mental math to add or subtract.

9. $40 + 70 =$ _____   10. $800 + 200 =$ _____

11. $90 + 60 =$ _____   12. $500 + 800 =$ _____

13. $1,600 - 900 =$ _____   14. $130 - 80 =$ _____

15. $1,500 - 700 =$ _____   16. $110 - 50 =$ _____

Homework

Subtract. Show your ungroupings. Use proof drawings if you need to.

1. $\begin{array}{r} 400 \\ -\ 341 \\ \hline \end{array}$

2. $\begin{array}{r} 700 \\ -\ 456 \\ \hline \end{array}$

3. $\begin{array}{r} 300 \\ -\ 118 \\ \hline \end{array}$

4. $\begin{array}{r} 500 \\ -\ 238 \\ \hline \end{array}$

5. $\begin{array}{r} 200 \\ -\ 47 \\ \hline \end{array}$

6. $\begin{array}{r} 800 \\ -\ 572 \\ \hline \end{array}$

7. $\begin{array}{r} 1{,}000 \\ -\ 345 \\ \hline \end{array}$

8. $\begin{array}{r} 2{,}000 \\ -\ 876 \\ \hline \end{array}$

9. $\begin{array}{r} 3{,}000 \\ -\ 905 \\ \hline \end{array}$

Solve each problem. Show your work. Make proof drawings if you need to.

Show your work.

10. Sasha had $4.00 to buy lunch. He spent $3.58. How much money does he have now?

_____

11. Jay's family will travel 1,000 miles during their summer trip. So far, they have traveled 567 miles. How many more miles must they go?

Name _____ **Date** _____

Remembering

Add.

1. 325	2. $4.95	3. 2,584	4. $35.68
+ 257	+ 2.67	+ 3,745	+ 13.95

Solve the word problems.

Show your work.

5. A zoo had 143 otters. They then got 45 more otters from another zoo. How many otters does the zoo have now?

_____

Dennis earned 102 dollars mowing lawns over the summer. In the winter, e earned 39 dollars shoveling d eways. How much did he earn in all

_____

7. There were 151 people in the audience when the concert began. After the first song, 46 more people came in. How many people were in the audience after the first song?

_____

8. Ji Young delivered 48 papers on Saturday and 105 papers on Sunday. How many papers did she deliver over the weekend?

_____

Subtract Across Zeros

Homework

Solve each problem. Use the ad for Andy's Arts and Crafts Store on Student Book page 34.

1. You have $5.00. If you buy a set of paints, how much will you have left? _____

2. You have $3.75. If you buy construction paper, how much will you have left? _____

3. You have $1.00. If you buy a marker, how much will you have left? _____

4. You have $6.00. If you buy a set of cookie cutters and glue, how much will you have left?

   _____

Subtract.

5. 972
   − 129

6. 300
   − 276

7. 1,278
   − 426

8. 1,336
   − 207

9. 1,398
   − 528

10. 997
   − 218

11. Write a word problem for one of the subtraction exercises above.

   _____

   _____

   _____

Remembering

Add.

1.	972	2.	309	3.	1,278	4.	449
	+ 129		+ 276		+ 426		+ 88

Use mental math to add or subtract.

5. $800 + 800 =$ _____   **6.** $70 + 70 =$ _____   **7.** $900 + 300 =$ _____

8. $40 + 70 =$ _____   **9.** $1,800 - 900 =$ _____   **10.** $120 - 60 =$ _____

11. $1,500 - 500 =$ _____   **12.** $170 - 80 =$ _____   **13.** $1,600 - 900 =$ _____

Solve. Label your answer.   *Show your work.*

14. At a meeting of the third, fourth, and fifth grades, there are 58 third-graders, 62 fourth-graders, and 59 fifth-graders. How many students are at the meeting?

_____

15. Jen sells 125 raffle tickets. Jen's sister sells 89 raffle tickets. Melanie sells 119 raffle tickets. How many raffle tickets did the three girls sell in all?

_____

Discuss Methods of Subtractings

Homework

Read each problem. Then follow the directions below the problem. Here is an addition word problem:

> At the arcade, Sanjay spent $2.75 playing video games and $1.49 on a bottle of water. How much did he spend altogether?

1. Solve the problem. _____

2. Write a subtraction word problem related to the addition word problem. Then find the answer without doing any calculations.

_____

_____

_____

_____

Here is a subtraction word problem:

> Rosi had 200 sheets of construction paper. She used 67 sheets making invitations to a party and the rest making decorations. How many sheets did she use to make decorations?

3. Solve the problem. _____

4. Write an addition word problem related to the subtraction word problem. Then find the answer without doing any calculations.

_____

_____

_____

Name _____ Date _____

Remembering

Add.

1. 654 + 112 = _____

2. 560 + 86 = _____

3. 66 + 284 = _____

4. 7 + 104 = _____

Add. Use mental math.

5. 30 + 420

6. 5 + 81 + 300

7. 206 + 40

_____

_____

_____

8. 60 + 317

9. 348 + 6

10. 348 + 90

_____

_____

_____

Solve each problem. Label your answer.

Show your work.

11. There are 265 people at the afternoon show. There are 387 people at the evening show. How many people were at the two shows?

_____

12. Jerry buys a turkey sandwich and a bottle of ice tea. The sandwich costs $4.29. The bottle of ice tea costs $1.35. How much money does Jerry spend in all?

_____

Relate Addition and Subtraction

Name _____ Date _____

Remembering

Solve each problem.
Make proof drawings if they help you.

Show your work.

1. At the start of the track meet, 375 people were in the stands. Then it started to rain, and 217 people left. How many people were still in the stands?

   _____

2. Samir had 378 marbles. He gave 152 of them to his little sister. How many marbles does Samir have now?

   _____

3. Samantha collected 714 basketball cards. She traded 281 of them for baseball cards. How many basketball cards does Samantha have left?

   _____

4. A thrift store had 173 hats for sale. A costume designer came in and bought 98 of the hats. How many hats were left?

   _____

5. Rosa went on vacation with her family. She traveled 219 miles by car and 476 miles by plane. How far did she travel?

   _____

Subtraction Practice

Ted's Toy Town

Beach Ball $3.45

Bat $5.75

Kite $2.99

Book of stickers $1.79

"Sorry Charlie"
board game $2.3

Use the ad to solve each problem.

1. Dion has $7.00. If he buys a bat, how much will he have left? _____

2. Manuela has $3.75. If she buys the "Sorry Charlie" board game, how much will she have left? _____

3. How much cheaper is the kite than the beach ball? _____

4. Imagine you have $10.00. Write down two items from the toy store ad, then find out how much money you would have left if you bought those two items.

   _____

   I would have _____ left.

5. On a separate sheet of paper, write and solve your own word problem using the toy store ad.

Name _____

Date _____

Homework

Solve.

1. Write and solve an addition word problem that has the numbers 268 and 487.

   _____

   _____

   _____

2. Write and solve a subtraction word problem that has the numbers 194 and 526.

   _____

   _____

   _____

3. The yearbook staff took a total of 1,005 photographs. They used 487 of the photographs in the yearbook. How many of the photographs were not used?

   _____

4. Mr. Pinsky has to read a 362-page book for his book club. He read the first 129 pages last week. This week he has read 153 pages. How many pages does he have left to read?

   _____

5. Josh had $9.00 in his pocket when he left the house this morning. He spent $1.75 on bus fare and $3.48 on lunch. How much does he have left?

   _____

Name _____ **Date** _____

Remembering

Solve.

Show your work.

1. Aimee's dog weighs 58 pounds and her cat weighs 13 pounds. How much do her dog and cat weigh together?

_____

2. Write a subtraction word problem related to the addition problem in Problem 1. Then solve the problem you wrote without doing any calculations.

_____

_____

Subtract. Check your answers by adding.

3. $1,163 - 793 =$ _____   4. $1,937 - 88 =$ _____   5. $627 - 329 =$ _____

Use mental math to find the answer.

6. $9 + 6 + 1 =$ _____   7. $5 + 7 + 2 =$ _____   8. $8 + 6 + 2 =$ _____

9. $40 + 20 + 30 =$ _____ 10. $60 + 60 + 60 =$ _____ 11. $70 + 40 + 20 =$ _____

12. $170 - 80 =$ _____   13. $140 - 50 =$ _____   14. $150 - 70 =$ _____

Addition and Subtraction Practice

Homework

Connections

Find a number in your neighborhood with 2 or 3 digits. It might be a house number or a number you see in the grocery store. Make a place-value drawing of the number.

Reasoning and Proof

Support or disprove this statement with examples: When you subtract one number from another, the answer is always less than both of the numbers in the subtraction problem.

_____

_____

_____

Communication

Franklin says the answer to the problem below is 48. Jill says the answer is 22. Who is right? Why?

$$\begin{array}{r} 35 \\ + 13 \\ \hline \end{array}$$

_____

_____

_____

Representation

Make place-value drawings of two different 3-digit numbers. Explain how the drawings show that the numbers have different values.

_____

_____

_____

_____

Remembering

Solve each problem.
Make proof drawings if they help you.

Show your work.

1. Kim had 243 stickers. She gave 120 away. How many stickers did she have left?

   _____

2. There were 125 people in one part of the theater and 154 people in another part of the theater. How many people were in the theater all together?

   _____

Subtract. Check your answers by adding.

3. $1{,}142 - 738 =$ _____

4. $638 - 572 =$ _____

5. $1{,}000 - 646 =$ _____

6. $1{,}519 - 510 =$ _____

7. $2{,}456 - 1{,}942 =$ _____

8. $3{,}217 - 2{,}106 =$ _____

Use mental math to find the answer.

9. $3 + 6 + 3 =$ _____

10. $1 + 5 + 9 =$ _____

11. $40 + 10 + 20 =$ _____

12. $20 + 20 + 20 =$ _____

Using Mathematical Processes

Find the perimeter of each triangle to the nearest centimeter.

1.
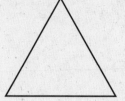

_____

2.

_____

Find the perimeter of each quadrilateral to the nearest centimeter.

3.
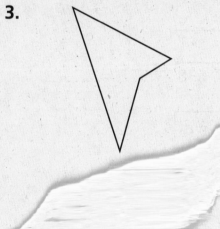

_____

4.

_____

5.
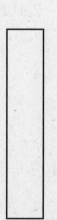

_____

6.

_____

Remembering

> Meg spent $3.75 on folders and $4.89 on notebooks. How much did she spend in all?

1. Solve the problem. _____

2. Write a subtraction word problem related to this addition word problem.

_____

_____

3. Find the solution to your subtraction problem without doing any calculations. _____

Explain. _____

_____

> Rodney had 122 butterflies in his collection. He gave 37 to his friend Jin. How many butterflies does he have now?

4. Solve the problem. _____

5. Write an addition word problem related to this subtraction word problem.

_____

_____

6. Find the solution to your addition problem without doing any calculations. _____

Explain. _____

_____

Name _____ **Date** _____

Homework

1. List all the pairs of adjacent sides in the quadrilateral.

   _____

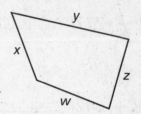

2. List all the pairs of opposite sides in the quadrilateral.

   _____

Tell whether each pair of lines is parallel, perpendicular, or neither.

3.

   _____

4.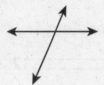

   _____

5.

   _____

6.

   _____

7. Name the perpendicular adjacent sides in the triangle.

   _____

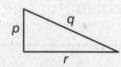

8. First draw a line segment 5 cm long. Then draw a line segment 7 cm long parallel to your first line segment.

9. Draw a triangle and label its sides _g_, _h_, and _i_. List all the pairs of adjacent sides in your triangle.

   _____

   _____

   _____

2-2

Remembering

Add or subtract. Use a separate sheet of paper.

1. 505 − 277 _____ **2.** 1,237 + 692 _____ **3.** 1,060 − 487 _____

4. 478 + 642 _____ **5.** 340 − 62 _____ **6.** 1,389 + 57 _____

7. 1,005 − 996 _____ **8.** 1,637 + 92 _____ **9.** 1,541 − 2 _____

10. 69 + 953 _____ **11.** 1,500 − 89 _____ **12.** 935 + 165 _____

13. Write a word problem for one of the addition exercises above.

_____

_____

_____

_____

_____

14. Write a word problem for one of the subtraction exercises above.

_____

_____

_____

_____

_____

Name _____ **Date** _____

Homework

Solve.

1. A square has sides 3 cm in length.

   What is the perimeter of the square? _____

2. The adjacent sides of a parallelogram have lengths of 12 cm and 18 cm.

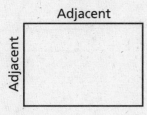
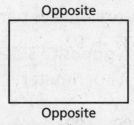

   What is the perimeter of the parallelogram? _____

3. Draw a rectangle that has sides 5 cm and 2 cm in length.

   What is the perimeter of your rectangle? _____

4. Draw a square with a perimeter of 8 cm.

5. Draw a parallelogram with a perimeter of 12 cm.

Remembering

Read each sentence and write whether it is true or false.

1. All squares are rectangles. _____

2. All parallelograms are squares. _____

3. All quadrilaterals are parallelograms. _____

4. The opposite sides of a square are always parallel. _____

5. If you know the lengths of two opposite sides of a parallelogram, you can find its perimeter. _____

Use the word problem below to complete exercises 6–8.

> Ms. Molina has 148 paperback books and 82 hardcover books. How many books does she have in all?

6. Solve the problem. _____

7. Write a subtraction word problem related to this addition word problem.

_____

_____

_____

8. Find the answer to your subtraction problem without doing any calculations.

_____

Parallelograms, Rectangles, Squares, and Rhombuses

Homework

Draw all the possible rectangles with a perimeter of 26 cm and whole-number lengths of sides. For each rectangle, label the lengths of two adjacent sides.

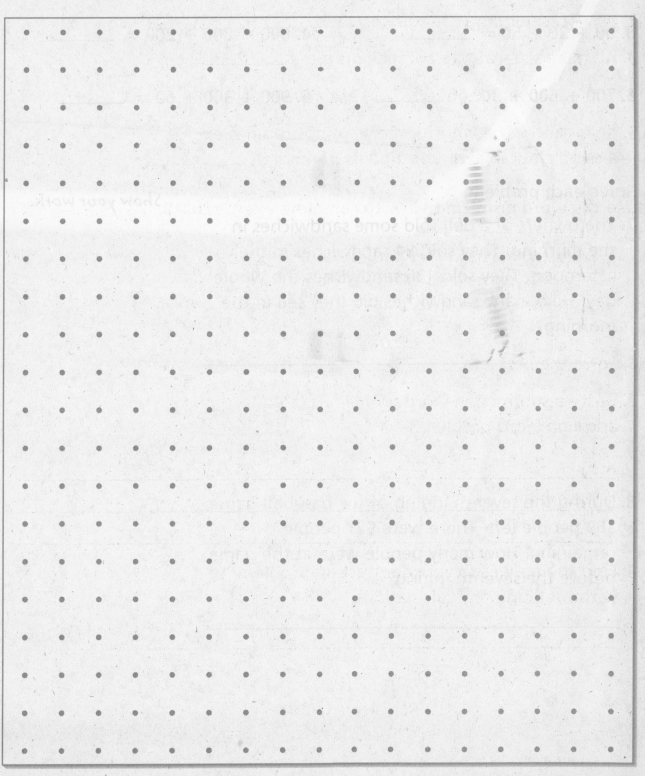

Name _____ **Date** _____

Remembering

Add using mental math. Write the answer.

1. 0 + 70 + 70 = _____

2. 40 + 80 + 20 = _____

3. 90 + 30 + 50 = _____

4. 600 + 800 + 200 = _____

5. 700 + 00 + 300 = _____

6. 900 + 300 + 50 = _____

Solve each problem.

Show your work.

7. The owners of a deli sold some sandwiches in the morning. They sold 84 sandwiches in the afternoon. They sold 30 sandwiches the whole day. How many sandwiches did they sell in the morning?

_____

8. During the seventh inning of the baseball game, 369 people left. There were 927 people remaining. How many people were at the game before the seventh inning?

_____

Draw Parallelograms and Rectangles

Circle every name that describes the figure.

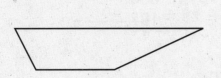   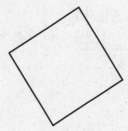   

1. quadrilateral

parallelogram

rectangle

square

2. quadrilateral

parallelogram

rectangle

square

3. quadrilateral

parallelogram

rectangle

square

Draw each figure if possible. If it is impossible to draw the figure, explain why it is impossible.

4. Draw a square that is *not* a quadrilateral.

5. Draw a quadrilateral that is *not* a square.

6. Draw a square that is *not* a parallelogram.

7. Draw a parallelogram that is *not* a square.

8. On a separate sheet of paper, sketch and label all possible rectangles with a perimeter of 30 cm and sides whose lengths are whole numbers.

Name _____ **Date** _____

Remembering

Add or subtract.

1. $\begin{array}{r} 682 \\ + 245 \\ \hline \end{array}$

2. $\begin{array}{r} \$6.94 \\ + 1.29 \\ \hline \end{array}$

3. $\begin{array}{r} 600 \\ - 187 \\ \hline \end{array}$

4. $\begin{array}{r} 877 \\ - 491 \\ \hline \end{array}$

5. $\begin{array}{r} 2,784 \\ + 3,725 \\ \hline \end{array}$

6. $\begin{array}{r} 4,562 \\ - 784 \\ \hline \end{array}$

Solve each problem.

Show your work.

7. Waleed barbecued some turkey burgers. He had 16 buns. He put a burger on each bun and had 5 buns left over. How many burgers did he cook?

   _____

8. The drama club sold too many tickets to the play. 782 people bought tickets. 37 people had to stand because there were not enough seats. How many seats are in the auditorium?

   _____

9. Sara had $5.00 to buy lunch. She spent $3.49. How much does she have left?

   _____

Classify Quadrilaterals

Name _____ **Date** _____

Homework

Draw a Math Mountain and write an equation to solve each problem.

Show your work.

1. **Change Plus** Kelsey had 9 books. She borrowed 4 more books from her friend. How many books does Kelsey have now?

   _____

2. **Change Minus** Write a subtraction problem that undoes the addition word problem in problem 1. Then draw a Math Mountain, write an equation, and solve the problem.

   _____

   _____

   _____

3. **Take Apart** There are 11 bicycles at Matt's house. 5 are in the driveway, and the rest are on the lawn. How many bicycles are on Matt's lawn?

   _____

4. **Put Together** Write an addition word problem that undoes the subtraction word problem in problem 3. Then draw a Math Mountain, write an equation, and solve the problem you wrote.

   _____

   _____

   _____

Write a number to make each number sentence true.

5. $17 = \boxed{} + 8$ 6. $\boxed{} \neq 9 - 4$ 7. $5 + 3 = 3 + \boxed{}$

Addition and Subtraction Situations **45**

Remembering

Unscramble the place values, and write the number for the words.

1. 8 tens + 3 hundreds + 5 ones _____

2. 1 thousand + 7 tens + 6 ones + 1 hundred _____

3. 8 hundreds + 4 ones + 1 thousand + 2 tens _____

Find the answer.

4. 387
      + 262

5. 491
      − 329

6. 588
      + 627

7. 45 + 22 + 16 = _____   **8.** 37 + 19 + 25 = _____

Solve each problem. Label your answer.

9. Julia went to camp with 4 friends. She made
7 new friends at camp. How many friends does
Julia have at camp now?

_____

10. Jen had 12 seeds to plant. She planted 3 of
them. How many seeds does she still have to
plant?

_____

Addition and Subtraction Situations

Name _____ **Date** _____

Homework

Solve each problem. Label your answers. _Show your work._

1. Asha made 15 sandwiches. Six were cheese, and the rest were peanut butter. How many peanut butter sandwiches did Asha make?

   _____

2. Farha has 13 CDs. She gave some of them to her sister. Now Farha has 5 CDs. How many did she give to her sister?

   _____

3. Joseph did 7 push-ups yesterday. Today he did some more. In all, he has done 14 push-ups. How many did he do today?

   _____

4. Devon read 8 chapter books and some picture books. Altogether he read 12 books. How many of them were picture books?

   _____

5. Brent has 14 models. 9 are airplane models and the rest are car models. How many are car models?

   _____

6. **Create and Solve** Write and solve a word problem in which you must find an unknown partner.

   _____

   _____

Remembering

Use a ruler to make each drawing.

1. Draw a horizontal line segment about 6 centimeters long.

2. Draw a vertical line segment a little more than 2 centimeters long.

3. Draw two perpendicular lines.

Add or subtract.

4. $926 + 158 =$ _____   **5.** $803 - 388 =$ _____   **6.** $687 - 79 =$ _____

Solve each problem. Label your answer.   *Show your work.*

7. Yolanda had $11. Then she spent some money on a magazine. She has $8 left. How much did she spend on the magazine?

_____

8. David is making a comic book. Last week, he finished the first 7 pages. This week, he finished some more pages. He has finished 12 pages in all. How many pages did he draw this week?

_____

Name _____ **Date** _____

Homework

Solve each problem. Label your answers.

Show your work.

1. At a farm, Brenna saw some cows. Then she saw 6 horses. She saw 15 cows and horses in all. How many cows did Brenna see?

   _____

2. Jamal caught some lightning bugs. His friend gave him 3 more. Now he has 9 lightning bugs. How many did he catch?

   _____

3. Anu is eating grapes. She has eaten 9 of them. She has 8 grapes left. How many grapes did she start with?

   _____

4. The school bus driver has brought 7 students home. 8 students are still on the bus. How many students were on the bus in the beginning?

   _____

5. Lana took some pictures at the zoo. She took 8 more pictures at the amusement park. She took 16 pictures altogether. How many pictures did she take at the zoo?

   _____

6. **Create and Solve** Write and solve an unknown start word problem of your own.

   _____

   _____

   _____

Name _____ **Date** _____

Remembering

Solve each problem. Label your answers.   *Show your work.*

1. The tiger at the zoo weighs 657 pounds. The brown bear weighs 763 pounds. How much do they weigh together?

   _____

   Miguel has saved 432 dollars. His friend Steve has saved 169 dollars. How much money have they saved in all?

   _____

Add or subtract.

3. 816 – 372 = _____   4. 783 – 194 = _____   5. 836 + 287 = _____

6. 782 – 553 = _____   7. 946 + 589 = _____   8. 900 – 179 = _____

9. Which figures are parallelograms? _____

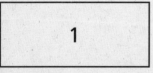 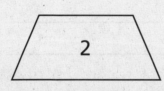  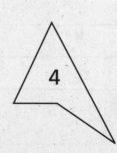

1   2   3   4

Problems with Unknown Starts

Homework

Solve each problem. Label your answers.

Show your work.

1. Unknown Difference Rex watched 14 movies over the summer. Luisa watched 8 movies. How many fewer movies did Luisa watch than Rex?

_____

2. Rewrite the question in Problem 1 using the word *more*.

_____

3. Unknown Smaller Amount Louis ate 14 crackers. Will ate 6 fewer crackers than Louis. How many crackers did Will eat?

_____

4. Unknown Larger Amount Raj walks 6 blocks to school. Zoe walks 5 more blocks than Raj. How many blocks does Zoe walk?

_____

Draw and label Comparison Bars to show each statement.

5. Travis has 7 fewer CDs than Bobbi has.

6. Ki solved 3 more math problems than Daniel solved.

7. Write another comparison statement for question 6.

_____

_____

Name _____ **Date** _____

Remembering

Add.

1. 97 + 43 + 17 = _____   **2.** 36 + 6 + 18 = _____

3. 112 + 218 + 160= _____   **4.** 324 + 48 + 162 = _____

5. Which figures are rectangles? Explain your answers.

 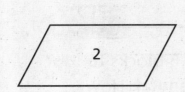  

_____

_____

Solve each problem. Label your answers.   _Show your work._

6. The 15 members of the Science Club went to the planetarium. Eight of the students rode in a van. The rest of the students rode in cars. How many students rode in cars?

_____

7. Ramona made some bracelets. She gave 8 of the bracelets away. Now Ramona has 5 bracelets left. How many bracelets did Ramona make?

_____

Comparison Problems

Homework

Solve each problem. Label your answers.   *Show your work.*

1. Lucia drew 13 pictures. Lucia drew 6 more pictures than Chelsea. How many pictures did Chelsea draw?

   _____

2. Derek brought 15 cupcakes to the party. After he gave one to each guest, he had 6 left. How many guests were at the party?

   _____

3. Molly hit 6 home runs. Molly hit 3 fewer home runs than Jerry. How many home runs did Jerry hit?

   _____

4. John caught 4 fireflies. He caught 6 fewer fireflies than Jessica. How many fireflies did Jessica catch?

   _____

5. Ankur ate 9 raisins. He ate 4 fewer raisins than Lena. How many raisins did Lena eat?

   _____

6. Amelia made 11 baskets. She made 3 more baskets than Girard. How many baskets did Girard make?

   _____

7. Roberto did 15 sit-ups. He did 5 fewer sit-ups than Marcus. How many sit-ups did Marcus do?

   _____

Name _____ **Date** _____

Remembering

Write whether each pair of line segments is parallel, perpendicular, or neither. Explain your answer.

1.

_____

_____

_____

2.

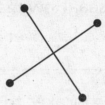

_____

_____

_____

3.

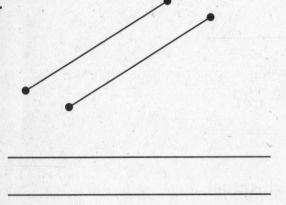

_____

_____

_____

4.

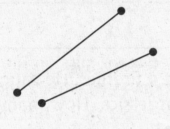

_____

_____

_____

Add or subtract.

5.	**6.**	**7.**	**8.**
367	398	701	827
+ 484	− 107	− 82	+ 394

Solve.

9. Raj brought $6.00 to the deli. He spent $2.67 on a turkey sub. How much money did he have left?

_____

Comparison Problems with Misleading Language

Homework

Solve each problem. Label your answers.

1. Trista used 872 beads to make some necklaces. There were 1,278 beads in the package to start. How many beads are left over?

_____

2. Ali is building a model boat from toothpicks. Yesterday, Ali used some toothpicks to start her model. Today, she added 398 toothpicks to finish the model. The finished model has 1,123 toothpicks. How many toothpicks did Ali use yesterday? _____

3. Collin received some hits on his new website yesterday. Today, he got 922 more hits. He now has 1,599 hits. How many hits did Collin get yesterday? _____

4. John went on a trip. The first day he traveled 489 miles. He traveled 261 miles the second day. How many miles did he travel? _____

5. Ronald and Tonya planted 542 flowers in all. Ronald planted 256 flowers. How many flowers did Tonya plant? _____

Write >, <, or = to make a true statement.

6. $4 + 3 + 2$ ___ $7 + 5$ **7.** 10 ___ $11 - 4$ **8.** 16 ___ $9 + 7$

Remembering

Subtract.

1. 500 − 377 = _____

2. 1,000 − 236 = _____

3. 400 − 32 = _____

4. 1,005 − 76 = _____

5. 300 − 18 = _____

6. 601 − 226 = _____

Solve.

7. Rusty had $6.00 to spend for lunch. He bought
a sandwich for $2.65, a banana for $0.78, and a
glass of juice for $1.89. How much money did
Rusty have left after he bought lunch?

_____

8. At the park, 8 children are playing tag and
10 are playing soccer. How many children are
playing tag or soccer in all?

_____

Complete.

9. A square is a rectangle that has _____.

10. A _____ is a quadrilateral in which both
pairs of opposite sides are parallel.

Multi-Digit Unknown Partner and Unknown Start Problems

Homework

Solve each problem. Label your answers.

1. A pet store has 231 bags of dog food. The store also has 543 bags of cat food. How many fewer bags of dog food does the store have than cat food? _____

2. At the spring concert, Tracy collected 561 tickets at the door. She collected 198 more tickets than Josie. How many tickets did Josie collect?

   _____

3. Victor has 647 trading cards. Victor has 179 fewer trading cards than Yan. How many trading cards does Yan have?

   _____

4. Stephanie baked 168 muffins for the bake sale. She also baked 288 cookies. How many more cookies did she bake than muffins?

   _____

5. Farmer Joe had 1,567 apple seedlings to plant. He put one seedling in each of the 1,072 holes he had dug. How many more holes does Farmer Joe need to dig? _____

Name _____

Date _____

Remembering

Measure the length of each line segment to the nearest centimeter.

1.  _____

2. _____

Use mental math to add or subtract. Write the answer.

3. 1,300 − 800 _____

4. 600 + 700 _____

5. 1,500 − 600 _____

6. 50 + 70 _____

7. 90 + 40 _____

8. 40 + 60 _____

Solve each problem. Label your answers.

> Jim wants to put his photos in albums. He has 425 photos. He can fit 100 in each album.

9. How many albums will Jim fill? _____

10. How many extra photos will he have? _____

Multi-Digit Comparison Problems

Solve each problem. Label your answers.

1. Tomas has 645 coins in his collection. Anna has
   862 coins. How many more coins does Anna
   have than Tomas? _____

2. There are 957 inner tubes at the water park.
   Everyone at the water park took one inner tube.
   There are 143 inner tubes left over. How many
   people are at the water park?

   _____

3. Miki and Jim are playing a board game.
   Together they have 545 points. Miki has scored
   255 points. How many points has Jim scored?

   _____

4. Rebecca has 125 books in her bookcase. She has
   93 fewer books than Paul. How many books
   does Paul have? _____

5. A cereal factory produced some boxes of cereal.
   The factory shipped 1,978 of the boxes to a
   supermarket. There are 1,265 of the boxes left
   at the factory. How many boxes of cereal did
   the factory produce? _____

Remembering

Find the perimeter of each figure to the nearest centimeter.

1.

_____

2.

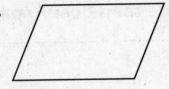

_____

3.

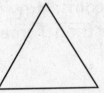

_____

Use mental math to add or subtract. Write the answer.

4. 30 + 60 + 50

_____

5. 80 + 60 + 20

_____

6. 70 + 40 + 70

_____

7. 700 + 400 + 300

_____

8. 200 + 900 + 300

_____

9. 600 + 300 + 500

_____

Solve.

10. Marissa brought 9 balloons to give one to each person at a picnic. 15 people came to the picnic. How many people did not get a balloon from Marissa?

_____

11. Today the mail carrier delivered 874 letters. She still has 279 letters in her truck to deliver. How many letters did she have in her truck at the beginning of the day?

_____

Mixed Multi-Digit Word Problems

Homework

Connections

This is a picture of Dave's garden.

6 ft

4 ft

Dave walks all the way around the garden. How far does he walk?

_____

Reasoning and Proof

Support or disprove with examples: All rectangles have 4 corners.

_____

Communication

Lupe had 13 marbles. She gave 7 marbles away. How many marbles does she have now?

Carol says Lupe has 20 marbles now. Chen says Lupe has 6 marbles now. Who is right? Why?

_____

_____

_____

Representation

Draw a picture to show this problem.

There are 6 people in a park. 3 more people come to the park. How many people are in the park now?

_____

Name _____ **Date** _____

Remembering

Measure the length of each line segment to the nearest centimeter.

1.

_____

2.

_____

Use mental math to add or subtract. Write the answer.

3. $60 + 70$ _____

4. $30 + 50$ _____

5. $400 + 900$ _____

6. $1,300 + 200$ _____

7. $1,100 + 800$ _____

8. $200 + 700$ _____

Solve.

9. Roberto has 7 marbles. His friend gives him 8 more marbles. How many marbles does he have now? _____

10. Jan gave away 24 flowers. After she gave away the flowers she still had 43 flowers left. How many flowers did she start with?

_____

Use Mathematical Processes

Name _____ **Date** _____

Homework

Draw all of the lines of symmetry for each figure.

1.

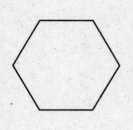

2.

3.

4.

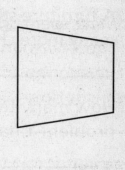

---

5. Which of the two figures below are congruent?

Figures _____ and _____ are congruent.

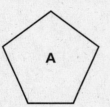 A
 B
 C
 D

---

6. Emma is making greeting cards for her classmates.
Circle the letter of each card that Emma can fold so
that the halves match exactly.

A   B   C   D   E

 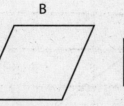 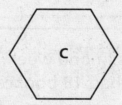 

---

7. How many lines of symmetry does the human body
have? Draw a stick figure and show the lines of
symmetry.

_____

Remembering

Solve.

Show your work.

1. A furniture store had 16 tables and 64 chairs. How many more chairs did the store have than tables?

_____

2. How many tables and chairs did the store in problem 1 have altogether?

_____

3. The store in problem 1 sold some chairs. Now there are 48 chairs. How many chairs did the store sell?

_____

4. The store sold 24 bookcases in one week. At the end of the week, the store had 18 bookcases left. How many bookcases did the store have at the start of the week?

_____

Find the perimeter of each triangle to the nearest centimeter.

5.

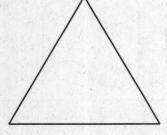 _____

6.

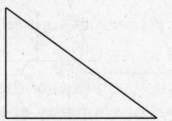 _____

7. Draw a rhombus that is not a square. Use *s* and *t* to label two adjacent sides. Use *u* to label the side opposite side *s*. Use *v* to label the fourth side.

Symmetry and Congruence

Homework

Use these figures to complete the exercises below.

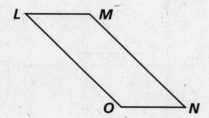

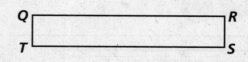

You may want to trace the figures and fold or cut out
the traced figures to check for symmetry and congruence.

1. Give two names for the parallelogram. _____ _____

2. Give two names for the rectangle. _____ _____

3. Draw diagonal *LN.* Is this diagonal a line of
   symmetry? _____

4. Name the two triangles formed when you drew
   diagonal *LN.* _____ _____
   Are these two triangles congruent? _____

5. Draw diagonal *TR.* Is this diagonal a line of
   symmetry? _____

6. Name the two triangles formed when you drew
   diagonal *TR.* _____ _____
   Are these two triangles congruent? _____

7. Draw diagonal *MO.* Are diagonals *LN* and *MO* the
   same length? _____

8. Draw diagonal *QS.* Circle the point in each quadrilateral
   where the two diagonals cross. Describe any congruent
   triangles formed by the diagonals.

   _____

Find the value of each collection of coins and bills.

1.

_____

2.

_____

3.

_____

4. List all the pairs of adjacent sides in the quadrilateral.

_____

5. List all the pairs of opposite sides in the quadrilateral.

_____

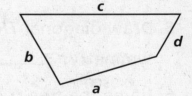

Write whether each pair of lines is parallel, perpendicular, or neither.

6.

_____

7.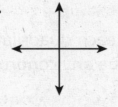

_____

8.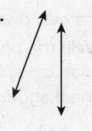

_____

9.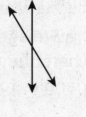

_____

Look at the angles below.

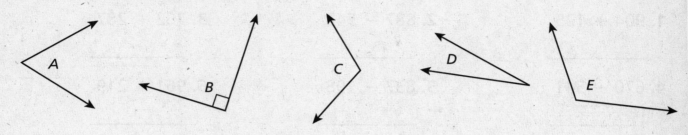

1. Which angles are right angles? _____

2. Which angles are obtuse angles? _____

3. Which angles are acute angles? _____

Mark all the words that describe each triangle.

4.

☐ equilateral
☐ isosceles
☐ scalene
☐ right
☐ acute
☐ obtuse

5.

☐ equilateral
☐ isosceles
☐ scalene
☐ right
☐ acute
☐ obtuse

6.

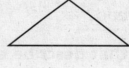

☐ equilateral
☐ isosceles
☐ scalene
☐ right
☐ acute
☐ obtuse

7.

☐ equilateral
☐ isosceles
☐ scalene
☐ right
☐ acute
☐ obtuse

On a separate sheet of paper, draw an example of each figure described below.

8. Equilateral–Acute triangle   **9.** Isosceles–Right triangle

10. Scalene–Obtuse triangle   **11.** Convex polygon

12. Pentagon   **13.** Hexagon

Remembering

Add or subtract.

1. 904 + 125

_____

2. 887 − 542

_____

3. 762 + 287

_____

4. 670 − 541

_____

5. 837 − 198

_____

6. 961 + 219

_____

Solve.

7. Fido ate 11 dog biscuits. Fido ate 4 more dog biscuits than Rover. How many dog biscuits did Rover eat?

_____

8. Zeke read 12 pages in his Social Studies textbook. He read 9 fewer pages than Kaya. How many pages did Kaya read?

_____

Mark all the names that describe each figure.

9.
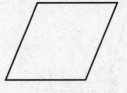

☐ quadrilateral
☐ parallelogram
☐ rhombus
☐ rectangle
☐ square

10.
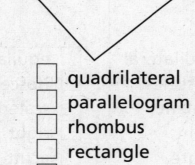

☐ quadrilateral
☐ parallelogram
☐ rhombus
☐ rectangle
☐ square

11.

☐ quadrilateral
☐ parallelogram
☐ rhombus
☐ rectangle
☐ square

Draw the lines of symmetry for each figure below.

12.
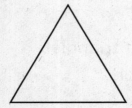

13.
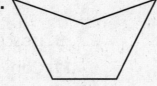

14.
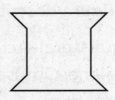

Angles and Triangles

Homework

What is the measure of each angle?

1. a right angle

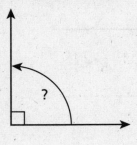

_____

2. 45° less than a straight angle

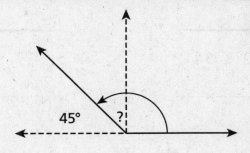

_____

3. 30° less than a right angle

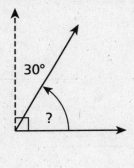

_____

4. 30° more than a straight angle

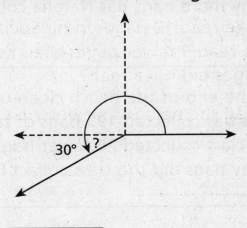

_____

Find the missing angle measure in each triangle.

5.

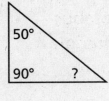

_____

6.

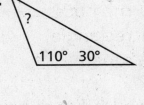

_____

7.

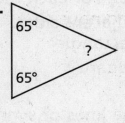

_____

8. A triangle has a 30°-angle and an angle that measures twice this amount. What is the measure of the triangle's third angle?

_____

Remembering

Add or subtract.

1. $89 + 175$ **2.** $1,900 - 899$ **3.** $30 + 1,055$

_____   _____   _____

Solve.

4. Natalie and Olivia are participating in the beach clean-up day. Natalie has collected 13 bags of trash. Olivia has collected 9 bags of trash. How many more bags has Natalie collected than Olivia?

_____

5. At the end of the beach clean-up day, Natalie's class has collected 193 bags of trash. Last year, her class collected 20 fewer bags of trash. How many bags did the class collect last year?

_____

6. Sketch all of the possible rectangles with a perimeter of 18 cm and whole-number lengths of sides. For each rectangle, label the lengths of two adjacent sides.

Homework

Solve by rounding to the nearest hundred.   *Show your work.*

1. On Friday, 718 people went to the school play. On Saturday, 822 people went. About how many people saw the play altogether?

   _____

2. So far, Ms. Sahid has read 177 pages of her 392-page book. About how many pages does she have left to read?

   _____

3. This year, the three biggest pumpkins at the Giant Pumpkin contest weighed 558 pounds, 644 pounds, and 715 pounds. About how much did the three pumpkins weigh together?

   _____

Round each number to the nearest hundred.

4. 352 _____   5. 620 _____   6. 298 _____

7. 539 _____   8. 1,014 _____   9. 769 _____

Use rounding to decide if the answer is reasonable.
Then find the answer to see if you were right.

10. $24 + 107 = 217$

    _____

12. $485 - 312 = 362$

    _____

14. $175 + 216 = 261$

    _____

11. $512 - 479 = 33$

    _____

13. $1,201 + 179 = 1,380$

    _____

15. $712 - 392 = 320$

    _____

Remembering

Solve each problem.   *Show your work.*

1. Maggie had some pairs of socks. Then she bought 5 new pairs of socks. She has 17 pairs now. How many pairs of socks did she have to start with?

   _____

2. Raj had some CDs. He gave 13 CDs to his friend. Now he has 47 CDs. How many CDs did Raj start with?

   _____

Add or subtract.

3. $12 + 18 + 15 =$ _____   4. $70 + 50 + 30 =$ _____

5. $34 + 21 + 35 =$ _____   6. $26 + 14 + 52 =$ _____

7. 1,234
   $-$ 829

8. 2,642
   $-$ 1,875

9. 3,452
   $+$ 5,987

Add or subtract. Use mental math.

10. $130 - 80 =$ _____   11. $1,100 - 700 =$ _____

12. $170 - 60 =$ _____   13. $1,600 - 600 =$ _____

14. $50 + 70 =$ _____   15. $800 + 400 =$ _____

Round to the Nearest Hundred

Name _____ **Date** _____

Homework

Round each number to the nearest ten.

1. 907 _____ **2.** 75 _____ **3.** 196 _____

Solve.

> Students buying lunch at Rockwell Elementary School yesterday chose either burritos or pizza. 185 students chose burritos and 252 chose pizza.

4. Estimate the number of students who bought lunch by rounding each number to the nearest hundred.

_____

5. Estimate how many students bought lunch by rounding each number to the nearest ten.

_____

6. Find the total number of students who bought lunch. Which of your estimates is closer to the actual total? Explain.

_____

_____

7. Draw a figure on a sheet of paper. Estimate how many pennies will fit inside the figure. Check your prediction using pennies.

_____

Use rounding to decide if the answer is reasonable. Then find the answer to see if you were right.

8. $57 - 39 = 81$ **9.** $143 - 74 = 69$ **10.** $155 + 36 = 161$

_____ _____ _____

Name _____   **Date** _____

Remembering

Solve each problem.   *Show your work.*

1. 564 fans attended Friday's game. 712 fans attended Saturday's game. How many fewer fans attended Friday's game than Saturday's game?

   _____

2. Ms. Peña brought 36 juice boxes to the class picnic. She gave a juice box to each student at the picnic. She had 8 juice boxes left over. How many students attended the picnic?

   _____

3. Jing has 23 baseball pennants. She has 7 more pennants than Max. How many pennants does Max have?

   _____

4. Jeri had 6 blank CDs. She recorded 10 songs on each CD. What was the total number of songs that Jeri recorded?

   _____

Tell whether each statement is true or false.

5. All squares are rectangles.   _____

6. All rectangles are squares.   _____

7. All quadrilaterals are parallelograms.   _____

8. All rectangles are parallelograms.   _____

Round to the Nearest Ten

Homework

Compare. Write >, <, or = in each ◯.

1. 765 ◯ 756

2. 3,467 ◯ 3,758

3. 2,014 ◯ 2,410

4. 8,462 ◯ 8,462

Write the numbers in order from least to greatest.

5. 92, 78, 82

6. 496, 424, 485

_____

_____

Compare. Write >, <, or = in each ◯.

7. 80 + 27 ◯ 52 + 55

8. 41 − 17 ◯ 64 − 35

9. 218 + 206 ◯ 27 + 427

10. 114 + 43 ◯ 21 + 133

11. 114 − 21 ◯ 456 − 378

12. 34 + 76 + 10 ◯ 51 + 43 + 26

Compare without calculating. Write > or < in each ◯.

13. 15 + 1 ◯ 15 − 1

14. 145 − 71 ◯ 58 + 13

15. 72 − 56 ◯ 68 + 17

16. 381 − 88 ◯ 246 + 61

Name _____ Date _____

Remembering

Solve each problem. *Show your work.*

1. 468 people attended the school musical on Friday night. 523 people attended the musical on Saturday afternoon. How many more people attended the Saturday show than the Friday show?

   _____

2. Manuel is reading a book with 72 pages. Today he read 47 pages. How many pages does Manuel have left to read?

   _____

3. Sam had some baseball cards. Then he bought 17 more. Now he has 118 cards. How many cards did Sam start with?

   _____

Add or subtract.

4. 21 + 13 + 17 = _____

5. 219 − 87 = _____

6. 2,018 + 138 = _____

7. 1,468 − 166 = _____

8. 36 + 121 + 17 = _____

9. 723 − 538 = _____

Compare Whole Numbers

Homework

Find the value of each collection of coins and bills.

1.

_____

2.

_____

Compare the two collections of coins and bills.
Write >, <, or = in the answer box.

3.

```
[coins]     □     [coins]
```

Solve each problem.

4. Hector wants to buy a pack of trading cards that
   costs $1.20. He has 2 quarters, 5 nickels, and
   6 dimes. Does he have enough money to buy the
   trading cards? Explain.

_____

5. Nasir has 3 nickels, 2 dimes, 5 quarters, and
   7 pennies. Jen has 6 dimes, 12 pennies, 1 quarter,
   and 8 nickels. Who has more money?

_____

Remembering

Add or subtract.

1. 1,007 − 668 = _____

2. 229 + 161 = _____

3. 35 + 65 + 27 = _____

4. 52 + 24 + 16 = _____

Solve.

5. Joan had some new pencils. She lost 5 of them and has 16 left. How many new pencils did Joan have to start with? _____

6. Adam caught 6 fish in the morning. Kent caught 7 more fish than Adam caught. How many fish did Kent catch? _____

7. Allegra is building a model from popsicle sticks. Yesterday, she used some popsicle sticks to start her model. Today, she used 398 popsicle sticks to finish it. Altogether, Allegra used 1,123 popsicle sticks. How many did she use yesterday? _____

8. At the fair, the clowns made 943 balloon animals. They gave one to each child at the fair. There were 119 balloon animals left. How many children came to the fair?

_____

Money Values

Homework

Snappy School Supplies

Find the total cost of the items. Then tell how you could pay for the items using the fewest bills and coins (quarters, dimes, nickels, or pennies).

Show your work.

1. $_____ two pencil boxes

   _____

2. $_____ three pencils

   _____

3. $_____ a book and a ruler

   _____

4. $_____ a backpack and a pencil

   _____

5. $_____ a pack of pens and a ruler

   _____

6. $_____ two pencils and a pencil box

   _____

Remembering

Round each number to the nearest ten.

1. 234 _____

2. 1,018 _____

3. 65 _____

4. 709 _____

Round each number to the nearest hundred.

5. 254 _____

6. 829 _____

7. 1,761 _____

8. 955 _____

Draw two coin combinations for each amount.

9. 68¢

10. $1.00

11. $0.34

12. 59¢

13. 92¢

14. $0.87

Represent Money Amounts in Different Ways

Homework

Beach Snack Shop

Find the amount of change by counting on. Draw the coins and bills you counted.

1. Rick paid for a basket of bread with three $1 bills. How much change did he get?

_____

2. Natalie paid for a juice box and raisins with a $5 bill. How much change did she get?

_____

3. Abdul paid for a banana and a carton of milk with three $1 bills. How much change did he get?

_____

Remembering

Draw two coin combinations for each amount.

1. 48¢

2. $0.74

3. 52¢

4. $0.88

5. Jason bought a t-shirt for $9.98 and a bottle of sun block for $1.25. He gave the clerk $15.00. How much change should he get?

_____

6. The Cruz family traveled 292 miles to the beach and then 218 miles to the campground. About how many more miles did they travel to the beach than to the campground?

_____

7. Draw two perpendicular line segments, one 6 centimeters long and one 2 centimeters long.

8. Draw two parallel lines.

Make Change

Homework

Round each amount first to the nearest dime and then to the nearest dollar.

	Rounded to the nearest dime	Rounded to the nearest dollar
1. $1.55	_____	_____
2. $3.27	_____	_____
3. $6.18	_____	_____
4. $5.90	_____	_____

Solve.

Show your work.

5. Emilio spent 95¢ on trading cards, 43¢ on a bag of peanuts, and 68¢ on a banana. Estimate the total amount he spent by rounding the prices to the nearest dime and adding. _____

Aaron and his sisters Sophie and Maggie want to combine their money to buy a tie for their father. Aaron has $4.53, Sophie has $6.19, and Maggie has $1.26. The tie costs $12. Aaron wants to estimate to decide if they have enough money.

6. How do you think Aaron should make his estimate? What estimate do you get if you use your method?

_____

_____

_____

7. Do Aaron and his sisters have enough to buy the tie? _____

Remembering

Solve each problem.   *Show your work.*

1. Amanda has 5 quarters, 4 dimes, 3 nickels and
   2 pennies. How much money does she have?

   _____

2. Alan has 5 dimes, 5 nickels, and 5 pennies. Bart
   has 3 nickels, 3 quarters, and 3 pennies. Who
   has more money?

   _____

3. Jan has 6 quarters, 3 dimes, 7 nickels, and
   9 pennies in her pocket. Shay has a dollar bill,
   4 dimes, 9 nickels, and 23 pennies in her
   pocket. Who has more money?

   _____

Round each number to the nearest ten.

4. 47 _____   5. 61 _____

6. 184 _____   7. 238 _____

8. 403 _____   9. 555 _____

**Draw two different ways to make $1.56 with bills
and coins.**

10.   11.

Name _____ **Date** _____

Homework

This table shows the number of tickets sold for the early and late showings of each movie at the Palace Theater last Saturday.

Saturday Ticket Sales

	Jungle Adventure	Hannah the Hero	Space Race
Early Show	72	109	143
Late Show	126	251	167

1. How many fewer tickets were sold for the early showing of *Jungle Adventure* than for the late showing?

_____

2. How many more tickets were sold for the late showing of *Hannah the Hero* than for the late showing of *Space Race*?

_____

This table shows the number of pizza, pasta, and salad orders at Luigi's Pizzeria last Tuesday and Wednesday.

Orders at Luigi's Pizzeria

	Pizza	Pasta	Salads
Tuesday	45	27	18
Wednesday	51	65	29

3. Write one addition question and one subtraction question based on the table above, and then find the answers.

_____

_____

_____

_____

Remembering

1. Draw a square with a perimeter of 12 centimeters.
   Label the sides with their lengths.

Round each amount first to the nearest dime and then to the nearest dollar.

	Nearest dime	Nearest dollar
2. $2.56	_____	_____
3. 67¢	_____	_____
4. $4.12	_____	_____
5. $3.94	_____	_____
6. $1.50	_____	_____

7. **Write Your Own** Using three of the money
   amounts above, write a word problem about
   how you are selling three items so that you can
   buy a book that costs $8.00. Solve your word
   problem by estimating.

   _____

   _____

   _____

   _____

   _____

Name _____

Date _____

Homework

1. This table shows how many calendars of each type the third graders ordered from the calendar publisher, the number they sold, and the number they have left. Fill in the empty cells.

Third Grade Calendar Sales

	Number Ordered	Number Sold	Number Left
Playful Puppies	475	387	
Adorable Kittens	300		177
Lovable Lambs		471	79

2. Make up a Comparison question about the table that uses the word *more*, and find the answer.

_____

_____

_____

3. This table shows the number of students at Lakeside Elementary who participate in various activities. Fill in the empty cells.

Participation in Activities

	Boys	Girls	Total
Band or Chorus	36	43	
Sports		78	171
After-School Clubs	47		86

4. Make up a Comparison question about the table that uses the word *fewer*, and write the answer.

_____

_____

Name _____

Date _____

Remembering

Solve.

1. Alicia had 419 coins in her collection. She gave 78 to her little brother. How many coins does she have now?

   _____

2. Write an addition word problem that undoes problem 1. Solve your word problem without doing any calculations.

   _____

   _____

   _____

   _____

3. On Saturday, a shoe store sold 278 pairs of women's shoes and 155 pairs of men's shoes. How many pairs of shoes did they sell in all?

   _____

4. Write a subtraction word problem that undoes problem 3. Solve your word problem without doing any calculations.

   _____

   _____

   _____

   _____

Complete Tables

Homework

> Sam and Zoe each tossed a coin. Here are their results:
>
> Sam: H H T H H T T H T H H H H H T T H T T
>
> Zoe: T H T H T T H H H T H T T T T H H H

1. Show the results in this table.

2. Write two questions that can be answered using your table, and give the answers.

_____

_____

_____

_____

Solve each problem.

3. This table shows how many bowls of soup Dee's Diner sold in three days. Fill in the empty cells.

Soup Sales for Dee's Diner

	Curly Noodle	Creamy Tomato	Total
Monday	104	132	
Tuesday	76		200
Wednesday		58	172

4. Write two Comparison word problems on another sheet of paper about the table in problem 3. Give the answers.

Remembering

Solve each problem.   *Show your work.*

1. Lauren's dog gained 7 pounds since his last visit to the vet. He weighs 54 pounds now. How much did he weigh on his last visit to the vet?

_____

2. Carlos's mom measures his height on every birthday. On his seventh birthday, he was 50 inches tall. This is 9 inches taller than he was on his fourth birthday. How tall was Carlos on his fourth birthday?

_____

3. Toshi lives 229 miles from her grandmother and 405 miles from her cousin Kioko. How much farther does Toshi live from her cousin than from her grandmother?

_____

Draw each shape if you can. If it is impossible to draw the shape, explain why it is impossible.

4. a quadrilateral that is not a rectangle

_____

5. a square that is not a parallelogram

_____

_____

_____

6. a parallelogram that is not a rectangle

_____

_____

_____

Solve each word problem. *Show your work.*

1. Galen had 75 toy cars and 98 building blocks. He gave 32 toy cars to his little brother. How many toy cars does Galen have left?

   _____

2. Isabelle baked a dozen muffins. Her family ate 5 of them. How many muffins does Isabelle have left?

   _____

3. Connie had 102 pennies, 4 dimes, and 3 nickels. How many cents did Connie have?

   _____

4. Guy ran 6 miles on Monday. He biked 13 miles on Wednesday. Then he ran 7 miles on Friday. How many miles did Guy run this week?

   _____

5. Quentin took a trip to China. It took him 2 days and 13 hours to get there. How many hours was Quentin traveling?

   _____

6. Tamika has a collection of 386 stamps. She has a collection of 137 figurines. She gave her mother 127 of her stamps. How many stamps does Tamika have now?

   _____

Name _____ **Date** _____

Remembering

Solve each word problem. *Show your work.*

1. Laci spent $4.29 on a squeaky toy, $2.69 on a box of dog biscuits, and $5.78 on a dog collar. By rounding each price to the nearest dollar, estimate how much Laci spent.

_____

2. In the election for school president, 188 people voted for Cameron, 243 people voted for Luke, and 410 people voted for Margo. By rounding each number to the nearest hundred, estimate the total number of voters.

_____

Find the value of each collection of money.

3.

_____

4.

_____

5.

_____

Word Problems with Extra or Hidden Information

Homework

Solve each problem if possible. If more information is needed, rewrite the problem and then solve it.

1. There are 15 children at a beach party. A dozen are eating watermelon. The rest are playing volleyball. How many children are playing volleyball?

   _____

   _____

   _____

2. There were 9 ducks and 8 geese on the pond. Then some of the ducks flew away. How many ducks were left?

   _____

   _____

   _____

3. Mark knitted 125 pairs of mittens to sell at the craft fair. He sold most of them. How many pairs of mittens did he have left?

   _____

   _____

   _____

4. Frederico brought 7 balloons, 12 rolls of red streamers, and some rolls of blue streamers to the party. How many rolls of streamers did he bring?

   _____

   _____

   _____

5. Explain how you would solve the problem below. If you cannot solve it, explain what other information you need to know to find the answer.

   > There were 20 legs on the animals in the pet shop. There were 2 dogs, 2 cats, and 1 other animal. The other animal was a lizard, a mouse, or a parrot. What was the other animal?

   _____

   _____

   _____

Remembering

Solve each problem.   *Show your work.*

1. Matt spent some time practicing the piano.
   Then he spent 25 minutes practicing the guitar.
   He spent a total of 60 minutes practicing. How
   much time did he practice the piano?

   _____

2. A vendor at the park sold 415 bottles of water
   on Saturday. She sold 137 fewer bottles of
   water than cups of lemonade. How many cups
   of lemonade did she sell?

   _____

3. The table shows the Bagel Shop's sales last
   Monday morning. Fill in the empty cells.

Monday Morning Bagel Sales

	Number Made	Number Sold	Number Left
Plain	420	385	
Cinnamon Raisin	336		128
Sesame		249	39
Onion	216		89

Write two Comparison questions that can be
answered by using the table. Give the answers.

4. _____

_____

5. _____

_____

       Word Problems with Not Enough Information

Homework

Solve each problem. Label your answers.

Show your work.

1. Todd's dad cut 12 slices of mango. Todd ate 4 of them. Then Todd's mom cut 6 more slices. How many slices of mango were left?

_____

2. Jennifer picked 3 daffodils, 9 daisies, and some tulips for her mother. Altogether she picked 16 flowers. How many tulips did she pick?

_____

3. Alex has 14 books in his bag. Angela has 6 fewer books in her bag than Alex has. How many books are in the two bags altogether?

_____

4. Pedro had 13 marbles yesterday. 7 were red, and the rest were green. Today he gave 4 of his green marbles to his sister. How many green marbles does Pedro have left?

_____

5. There were 17 animals at the shelter. 8 were dogs, and the rest were cats. Today more cats were brought in. Now there are 11 cats. How many cats were brought to the shelter today?

_____

6. Zal picked 12 cherries from one tree and 3 from another. He picked 8 more cherries than Karen picked. How many cherries did Karen pick?

_____

Remembering

Tell how to represent each amount with the _fewest_ coins (quarters, dimes, nickels, and pennies) possible.

1. 99¢ _____

2. $0.32 _____

3. 72¢ _____

4. $0.66 _____

Find the missing number.

5. 337 + $\boxed{}$ = 423

6. $\boxed{}$ + 246 = 523

7. 703 − $\boxed{}$ = 419

8. $\boxed{}$ − 86 = 235

9. This table shows the number of sheets of construction paper the art teacher had at the beginning of the year, the number students used, and the number left at the end of the year. Fill in the empty cells.

Construction Paper Supply

	Sheets at Start of Year	Sheets Used	Sheets Left
Red	1,250	933	
Yellow	1,000		323
Blue		1,096	404
Orange	750	556	

Solve Two-Step Word Problems

Homework

Solve each problem. Label your answers.

Show your work.

1. Jamika is packing for camp. In one suitcase, she packed 6 shirts, 7 pairs of shorts, 4 pairs of pants, and 2 caps. Later she decided to take out 3 pairs of the shorts. How many pieces of clothing are in Jamika's suitcase now?

   _____

2. Fabiola had $5.35, and Jay had $6.94. Fabiola spent $3.75, and Jay spent $4.87. Who has more money now? How much more?

   _____

3. Mira had a dozen white eggs and a dozen brown eggs in her refrigerator. She used 5 white eggs and 9 brown eggs to make a dessert. Altogether, how many eggs does she have left?

   _____

4. Ms. Luong made 17 copies of her math test. Then she made 8 more copies. She made 6 fewer copies of her test than Mr. Dorn made of his test. How many copies did Mr. Dorn make?

   _____

5. Sandra and Lana baked two kinds of muffins for the school bake sale. Sandra baked 18 blueberry muffins and 24 raisin muffins. Lana baked 24 more blueberry muffins and 12 fewer raisin muffins than Sandra baked. How many muffins did Lana bake?

   _____

Remembering

Round each value to the nearest dollar.

1. $3.50   **2.** $2.15   **3.** $7.87

_____   _____   _____

4. $9.79   **5.** $4.09   **6.** $5.33

_____   _____   _____

7. The table shows the number of pairs of glasses and
contact lenses an optician sold over three months.
Fill in the empty cells.

Sales at Optical World

	Glasses	Contacts	Total
May	74	132	
June	109		214
July		83	151

8. Write a comparison question using the data in the
table above and the word *fewer.* Answer your question.

_____

_____

9. Write an addition question about this table.

_____

_____

_____

Homework

Use the horizontal bar graph to answer each question.

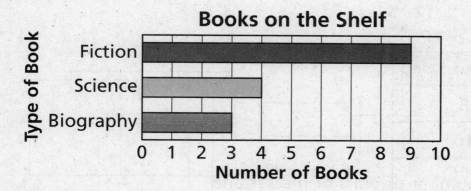

Books on the Shelf

Type of Book: Fiction, Science, Biography — Number of Books (0 1 2 3 4 5 6 7 8 9 10)

1. How many fiction books are on the shelf? _____

2. How many more science books are there on the shelf than
   biographies? _____

3. Write two of your own questions that can be answered
   using the graph.

   _____

   _____

Use the vertical bar graph to answer each question.

The Jacobs Family's Pets

4. How many cats and dogs does the Jacobs
   family have in all? _____

5. Which type of pet does the Jacobs family
   have the fewest of? _____

6. Write two of your own questions that can
   be answered using the graph.

   _____

   _____

Number of Pets (0–8) — Type of Pet: Dog, Fish, Cat

Name _____ **Date** _____

Remembering

1. Use the information in this table to make a horizontal bar graph.

Rashid's Hours of Sleep

Day	Hours of Sleep
Monday	8
Tuesday	10
Wednesday	7

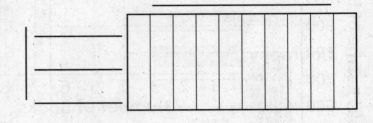

Show your work.

Solve each problem if you can. If you don't have enough information to solve it, tell what else you would need to know.

2. Ann's family went on vacation for a week and 4 days. Tye's family went on vacation for two weeks. How many days longer was Tye's vacation than Ann's?

_____

3. Last week, a clothing store sold 113 short-sleeve shirts, 209 long-sleeve shirts, 263 pairs of pants, and 78 pairs of shorts. How many more pants did they sell than shorts?

_____

4. A gallery had 47 paintings, 75 photographs, and some sculptures. How many more paintings did the gallery have than sculptures?

_____

Solve each equation.

5. $266 + \boxed{} = 321$ 6. $\boxed{} - 55 = 27$ 7. $400 - \boxed{} = 143$

Read and Create Bar Graphs

Name _____ **Date** _____

Homework

Use the vertical bar graph to answer the questions.

Sunnytown Reading Festival

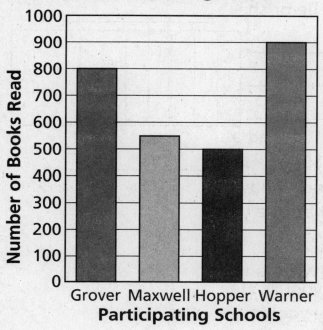

1. About how many books did students at Maxwell School read?

_____

2. At which school did students read the most books?

_____

3. How many fewer books did students at Hopper School read than students at Warner School?

_____

4. On a separate sheet of paper, write two of your own questions that can be answered using the bar graph.

5. Use the information in this table to make a vertical bar graph.

Pinball Scores

Player	Points
Trina	500
Mindy	350
Warren	200

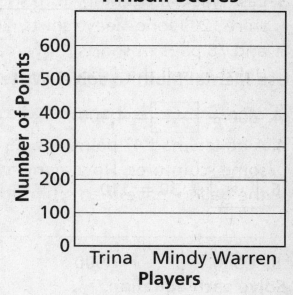

Pinball Scores

Remembering

Solve each problem. Label your answers.

Show your work.

1. Tyler has 5 quarters, 2 dimes, and 9 nickels. Jen has 3 quarters, 7 dimes, and 5 nickels. Who has more money? How much more does he or she have?

   _____

2. Zeynep bought a bowl of soup for $1.89 and a sandwich for $2.25. She paid with a $5 bill. How much change did she receive?

   _____

3. Josh had 6 containers of strawberry yogurt. He had 7 fewer containers of strawberry yogurt than blueberry yogurt. Then he ate 2 containers of blueberry yogurt. How many containers of blueberry yogurt does he have now?

   _____

Use Mental Math to solve. Write the answer.

4. $600 + \boxed{} = 1{,}100$

5. $70 + \boxed{} = 160$

6. $\boxed{} + 30 = 110$

7. $\boxed{} - 50 = 80$

8. $1{,}300 - \boxed{} = 900$

9. $\boxed{} - 400 = 1{,}200$

Read and Create Bar Graphs with Multi-Digit Numbers

Homework

Use the data to make a frequency table.

1.

Touchdowns Scored Last Season			
John	3	Bill	2
Samantha	0	Jason	4
Charles	3	Denzell	3
Jack	4	Rachel	2
Timothy	1	Jessica	0
Michelle	6	David	3
Patricia	5	Juan	5

Touchdowns Scored Last Season	
Number of Touchdowns	Number of Players

Use the data above to make a line plot.

2.

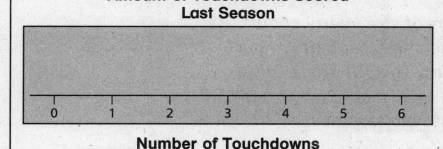

Amount of Touchdowns Scored Last Season

0   1   2   3   4   5   6

Number of Touchdowns

Use the data displays to answers the questions.

3. What is the range of the data? _____

4. What is the mode of the data? _____

5. How many players scored exactly 2 touchdowns? _____

6. How many players scored fewer than 3 touchdowns? _____

7. How many players scored more than 3 touchdowns? _____

Remembering

Round each value to the nearest dollar.

1. $3.48 _____

2. $2.55 _____

3. $16.50 _____

Find the missing number.

4. 336 + ☐ = 896

5. 1,865 − 746 = ☐

6. 277 + 345 = ☐

Find the value of each collection of money.

7.

_____

8.

_____

9.

_____

Homework

Connections

Make a timeline of what you did today at the bottom of the page.

Reasoning and Proof

Support or disprove with examples: All triangles are symmetrical.

_____

_____

Communication

At the zoo there are 3 bears, 5 tigers, and 4 lions. Write a word problem about the zoo. Give the answer to your problem.

_____

_____

_____

_____

Representation

Alma has 1 penny, 1 nickel, 1 dime, and 1 quarter in her purse. Suppose she takes 3 coins out of her purse. Draw a picture of the different possibilities.

Remembering

Solve each problem if you can. If you don't have enough information to solve it, tell what else you would need to know.

Show your work.

1. Dora has a dog that is 26 inches high.
   Sam has a dog that is 2 feet high.
   Whose dog is taller? How much taller?

   _____

   _____

2. There were 52 people in the movie theater. How many seats were empty?

   _____

   _____

   _____

Use mental math to solve. Write the answer.

3. $30 + \boxed{} = 120$

4. $\boxed{} + 400 = 1{,}200$

5. $\boxed{} + 50 = 130$

6. $130 - \boxed{} = 60$

7. $1{,}400 - \boxed{} = 500$

8. $\boxed{} - 200 = 1{,}100$

9. $\boxed{} + 20 = 20$

10. $25 + 42 = 42 + \boxed{}$

11. $3 + (4 + 7) = (\boxed{} + 4) + 7 = \triangle$

12. $(64 + 48) + 36 = (64 + 36) + \boxed{} = \triangle$

Use Mathematical Processes

Homework

Draw the new figure.

1. Show a half turn.

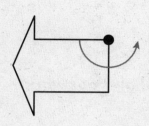

2. Show a flip.

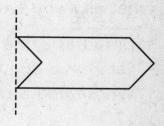

3. Show a slide.

4. Show a quarter turn.

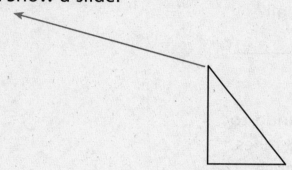

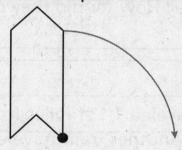

5. Show a flip.

6. Show a half turn.

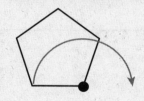

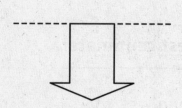

7. Show a flip.

8. Show a slide.

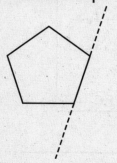

Remembering

Add or subtract.

1. 3,649
+ 1,326

2. 5,609
− 1,295

3. 8,457
+ 1,373

4. 4,517
− 1,242

Solve.

Show your work.

5. The Robinsons drove 1,356 miles the first week. The next week they drove another 1,172 miles. How far did they drive in all?

_____

6. A train traveled 1,131 miles from Orlando to Houston. Another train traveled 2,658 miles from Orlando to Palm Springs. How much farther did the second train travel?

_____

Find the perimeter of each quadrilateral to the nearest centimeter.

7.

8.

_____   _____

Motion Geometry Patterns

Homework

Write the next 3 numbers in the pattern.

1. 9 8 7 9 8 7 9 8 7 9 8 7 9 8 _____ _____ _____

2. 1 0 1 1 0 1 1 0 1 1 0 1 1 0 1 _____ _____ _____

3. 6 6 1 1 1 6 6 1 1 1 6 6 1 1 _____ _____ _____

4. 1 2 3 4 3 2 1 2 3 4 3 2 1 2 _____ _____ _____

Draw the next figure in the pattern.

5. 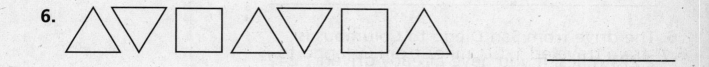 _____

6. 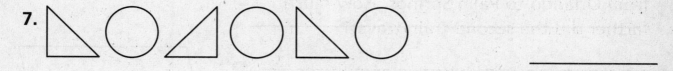 _____

7. 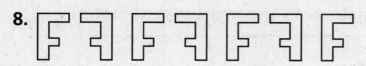 _____

How will you move the last figure to continue the pattern: slide, flip, or turn? Draw the next figure in the pattern.

8.  _____

9.  _____

10. 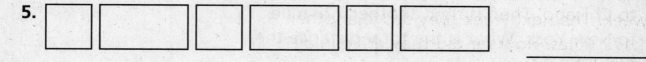 _____

Name _____ **Date** _____

Remembering

Add or subtract.

1. 7,521
   + 2,457

2. 9,999
   − 3,710

3. 3,207
   + 1,147

4. 2,683
   − 1,317

Solve.

Show your work.

5. A plane flew 1,718 miles from Los Angeles to Chicago. Then it flew another 728 miles to New York. What is the total distance the plane flew?

_____

6. The drive from San Diego to Columbus is 2,271 miles. If you have already driven 1,242 miles, how much farther do you have to go?

_____

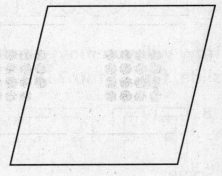

7. Name the figure on the right.

_____

8. Label two opposite sides *x* and *y*.

9. Draw a diagonal.

10. Is the diagonal a line of symmetry? Explain how you know.

_____

_____

_____

Repeating Patterns

Name _____

Date _____

Homework

Write the next two numbers in each pattern. Write the pattern rule.

1. 4, 9, 14, 19, 24, 29, _____ _____

Rule: _____

2. 100, 97, 94, 91, 88, 85, _____ _____

Rule: _____

3. 1, 10, 11, 20, 21, 30, _____ _____

Rule: _____

4. 100, 99, 97, 94, 90, 85, _____ _____

Rule: _____

Write the number of dots in each figure.
Then draw the next figure in each pattern.

5.

_____ _____ _____ _____

6.

_____ _____ _____ _____

Solve.

7. A book has pages numbered 1 to 50.
How many times is the digit 1 used in the
page numbers?

_____

Name _____ **Date** _____

Remembering

Add or subtract.

1.	5,870	2.	7,575	3.	2,294	4.	7,208
	+ 3,455		− 3,434		+ 5,827		− 2,914

Solve.

5. What is the greatest 4-digit number you can make with the digits 0, 1, 2, and 3?   _____

6. What is the least 4-digit number you can make with the digits 2, 4, 3, 1?   _____

Does the dashed line divide the figure into congruent halves? Write *yes* or *no*.

7. 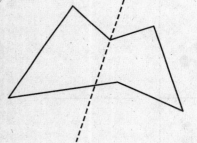   _____

8. 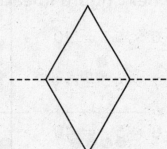   _____

Draw an isoceles, right triangle.

9.

Growing and Shrinking Patterns

Homework

Use this chart to practice your 5s count-bys and multiplications. Then have your Homework Helper test you.

	In Order	Mixed Up
5s	$1 \times 5 = 5$	$9 \times 5 = 45$
	$2 \times 5 = 10$	$5 \times 5 = 25$
	$3 \times 5 = 15$	$2 \times 5 = 10$
	$4 \times 5 = 20$	$7 \times 5 = 35$
	$5 \times 5 = 25$	$4 \times 5 = 20$
	$6 \times 5 = 30$	$6 \times 5 = 30$
	$7 \times 5 = 35$	$10 \times 5 = 50$
	$8 \times 5 = 40$	$8 \times 5 = 40$
	$9 \times 5 = 45$	$1 \times 5 = 5$
	$10 \times 5 = 50$	$3 \times 5 = 15$

7–1

Homework

Solve each equation. Then check your answers at the bottom of this page.

1. $8 \times 5 = \boxed{}$

2. $9 \cdot 5 = \boxed{}$

3. $5 * 2 = \boxed{}$

4. $6 \times 5 = \boxed{}$

5. $3 \cdot 5 = \boxed{}$

6. $5 \times 4 = \boxed{}$

7. $10 \times 5 = \boxed{}$

8. $5 * 1 = \boxed{}$

9. $6 \times 5 = \boxed{}$

10. $5 * 5 = \boxed{}$

11. $5 \cdot 7 = \boxed{}$

12. $2 * 5 = \boxed{}$

13. $5 * 1 = \boxed{}$

14. $5 \times 10 = \boxed{}$

15. $4 \cdot 5 = \boxed{}$

16. $7 \cdot 5 = \boxed{}$

17. $5 \times 2 = \boxed{}$

18. $5 * 7 = \boxed{}$

19. $5 \times 5 = \boxed{}$

20. $5 * 8 = \boxed{}$

21. $9 \cdot 5 = \boxed{}$

1. 40 **2.** 45 **3.** 10 **4.** 30 **5.** 15 **6.** 20 **7.** 50 **8.** 5 **9.** 30 **10.** 25
11. 35 **12.** 10 **13.** 5 **14.** 50 **15.** 20 **16.** 35 **17.** 10 **18.** 35 **19.** 25
20. 40 **21.** 45

Homework

Study Plan

Homework Helper

Write each total.

1. $2 \times \boxed{5} = 5 + 5 =$ _____

2. $4 \cdot \boxed{5} = 5 + 5 + 5 + 5 =$ _____

3. $6 * \boxed{5} = 5 + 5 + 5 + 5 + 5 + 5 =$ _____

**Write the 5s additions that show each multiplication.
Then write the total.**

4. $3 \times \boxed{5} =$ _____ $=$ _____

5. $5 * \boxed{5} =$ _____ $=$ _____

6. $1 \cdot \boxed{5} =$ _____ $=$ _____

7. $8 \cdot \boxed{5} =$ _____ $=$ _____

8. $7 \times \boxed{5} =$ _____ $=$ _____

Name _____ Date _____

Remembering

Add or subtract.

1. 836 − 421 = _____

2. 378 + 448 + 271 = _____

Use mental math to add or subtract.

3. 60 + 100 = _____

4. 500 − 80 = _____

5. 600 + 200 = _____

Solve each problem.

Show your work.

6. Carrie picked 8 carrots from her garden. Then she picked 6 more. How many carrots did Carrie pick in all?

_____

7. On Tuesday, the workers at the Tidy Pet Salon groomed 126 dogs. On Wednesday, they groomed 167 dogs. How many fewer dogs did they groom on Tuesday than on Wednesday?

_____

8. Darren packed a picnic basket. He packed 5 sandwiches, 8 boxes of juice, 6 bags of pretzels, and 5 apples. Later he took 3 bags of pretzels out of the basket. How many items were in the basket then?

_____

9. Marlena had 379 baseball cards. Then her brother gave her 122 more. How many baseball cards does she have now?

_____

Multiply with 5

Homework

Study Plan

_____

Homework Helper

Write a multiplication equation to show how many.

1. How many apples?

_____

2. How many lenses?

_____

Make a math drawing and label it. Write a multiplication equation that gives the answer.

3. Beth put the dinner rolls she baked in 5 bags, with 6 rolls per bag. How many rolls did Beth bake?

_____

4. Baya arranged her pennies into 7 piles of 5. How many pennies did she have?

_____

Multiplication as Repeated Groups **117**

Remembering

Circle every name that describes the figure.

1.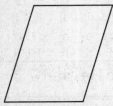

quadrilateral
parallelogram
rectangle
square

2.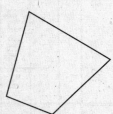

quadrilateral
parallelogram
rectangle
square

3.

quadrilateral
parallelogram
rectangle
square

4.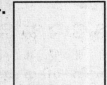

quadrilateral
parallelogram
rectangle
square

5.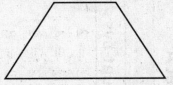

quadrilateral
parallelogram
rectangle
square

6.

quadrilateral
parallelogram
rectangle
square

Add or subtract.

7. $1,280 + 449 = $ _____

8. $1,809 - 622 = $ _____

9. $724 - 189 = $ _____

10. $463 + 782 = $ _____

Homework

Home Study Sheet A

5s

Count-bys	Mixed Up ×	Mixed Up ÷
1 × 5 = 5	2 × 5 = 10	10 ÷ 5 = 2
2 × 5 = 10	9 × 5 = 45	35 ÷ 5 = 7
3 × 5 = 15	1 × 5 = 5	50 ÷ 5 = 10
4 × 5 = 20	5 × 5 = 25	5 ÷ 5 = 1
5 × 5 = 25	7 × 5 = 35	20 ÷ 5 = 4
6 × 5 = 30	3 × 5 = 15	15 ÷ 5 = 3
7 × 5 = 35	10 × 5 = 50	30 ÷ 5 = 6
8 × 5 = 40	6 × 5 = 30	40 ÷ 5 = 8
9 × 5 = 45	4 × 5 = 20	25 ÷ 5 = 5
10 × 5 = 50	8 × 5 = 40	45 ÷ 5 = 9

2s

Count-bys	Mixed Up ×	Mixed Up ÷
1 × 2 = 2	7 × 2 = 14	20 ÷ 2 = 10
2 × 2 = 4	1 × 2 = 2	2 ÷ 2 = 1
3 × 2 = 6	3 × 2 = 6	6 ÷ 2 = 3
4 × 2 = 8	5 × 2 = 10	16 ÷ 2 = 8
5 × 2 = 10	6 × 2 = 12	12 ÷ 2 = 6
6 × 2 = 12	8 × 2 = 16	4 ÷ 2 = 2
7 × 2 = 14	2 × 2 = 4	10 ÷ 2 = 5
8 × 2 = 16	10 × 2 = 20	8 ÷ 2 = 4
9 × 2 = 18	4 × 2 = 8	14 ÷ 2 = 7
10 × 2 = 20	9 × 2 = 18	18 ÷ 2 = 9

10s

Count-bys	Mixed Up ×	Mixed Up ÷
1 × 10 = 10	1 × 10 = 10	80 ÷ 10 = 8
2 × 10 = 20	5 × 10 = 50	10 ÷ 10 = 1
3 × 10 = 30	2 × 10 = 20	50 ÷ 10 = 5
4 × 10 = 40	8 × 10 = 80	90 ÷ 10 = 9
5 × 10 = 50	7 × 10 = 70	40 ÷ 10 = 4
6 × 10 = 60	3 × 10 = 30	100 ÷ 10 = 10
7 × 10 = 70	4 × 10 = 40	30 ÷ 10 = 3
8 × 10 = 80	6 × 10 = 60	20 ÷ 10 = 2
9 × 10 = 90	10 × 10 = 100	70 ÷ 10 = 7
10 × 10 = 100	9 × 10 = 90	60 ÷ 10 = 6

9s

Count-bys	Mixed Up ×	Mixed Up ÷
1 × 9 = 9	2 × 9 = 18	81 ÷ 9 = 9
2 × 9 = 18	4 × 9 = 36	18 ÷ 9 = 2
3 × 9 = 27	7 × 9 = 63	36 ÷ 9 = 4
4 × 9 = 36	8 × 9 = 72	9 ÷ 9 = 1
5 × 9 = 45	3 × 9 = 27	54 ÷ 9 = 6
6 × 9 = 54	10 × 9 = 90	27 ÷ 9 = 3
7 × 9 = 63	1 × 9 = 9	63 ÷ 9 = 7
8 × 9 = 72	6 × 9 = 54	72 ÷ 9 = 8
9 × 9 = 81	5 × 9 = 45	90 ÷ 9 = 10
10 × 9 = 90	9 × 9 = 81	45 ÷ 9 = 5

Home Signature Sheet

	Count-Bys Homework Helper	Multiplications Homework Helper	Divisions Homework Helper
0			
1			
2			
3			
4			
5			
6			
7			
8			
9			
10			

Homework

Write a multiplication equation for each array.

1. How many muffins?

_____

2. How many basketballs?

_____

Make a math drawing for the problem and label it.
Write a multiplication equation that gives the answer.

3. Ellie arranged her trophies in 3 rows, with 6
   trophies in each row. How many trophies does
   she have?

_____

4. Maribel planted a garden with 9 tomato plants
   in each of 2 rows. How many tomato plants did
   she plant?

_____

Name _____

Date _____

Remembering

Solve each problem.

Show your work.

1. Lin has 13 baseball caps. Cameron has 5 fewer baseball caps than Lin. How many baseball caps does Cameron have?

_____

2. Today the hardware store sold 112 boxes of nails. At the end of the day, 136 boxes of nails were left. How many boxes of nails did the hardware store have at the beginning of the day?

_____

3. Jenna earned $217 delivering newspapers. She earned $132 washing cars. Then she bought a pair of roller blades for $75. How much money does Jenna have left?

_____

Use the bar graph to solve each problem.

4. If you have $5.00, how many more Yellow Point pencils can you buy than True Write pencils?

_____

5. How many Mark Right pencils can you buy for $10.00?

_____

6. How many fewer Always Sharp pencils can you get for $5.00 than Yellow Point pencils?

_____

7. Write a problem using the information in the bar graph. Solve your problem.

_____

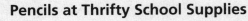

Pencils at Thrifty School Supplies

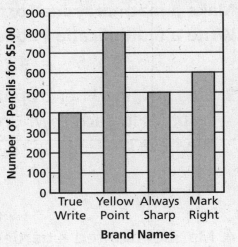

Number of Pencils for $5.00

900
800
700
600
500
400
300
200
100
0

True Write, Yellow Point, Always Sharp, Mark Right

Brand Names

Multiplication and Arrays

Homework

Use this chart to practice your 5s count-bys, multiplications, and divisions. Then have your Homework Helper test you.

	In Order ×	Mixed Up ×	Mixed Up ÷
5s	$1 \times 5 = 5$	$4 \times 5 = 20$	$20 \div 5 = 4$
	$2 \times 5 = 10$	$7 \times 5 = 35$	$5 \div 5 = 1$
	$3 \times 5 = 15$	$2 \times 5 = 10$	$50 \div 5 = 10$
	$4 \times 5 = 20$	$5 \times 5 = 25$	$35 \div 5 = 7$
	$5 \times 5 = 25$	$9 \times 5 = 45$	$15 \div 5 = 3$
	$6 \times 5 = 30$	$1 \times 5 = 5$	$45 \div 5 = 9$
	$7 \times 5 = 35$	$10 \times 5 = 50$	$10 \div 5 = 2$
	$8 \times 5 = 40$	$3 \times 5 = 15$	$25 \div 5 = 5$
	$9 \times 5 = 45$	$6 \times 5 = 30$	$40 \div 5 = 8$
	$10 \times 5 = 50$	$8 \times 5 = 40$	$30 \div 5 = 6$

Name _____ **Date** _____

Multiply or divide to find the unknown numbers.
Then check your answers at the bottom of this page.

1. $5 \times 6 = \boxed{}$

2. $45 \div 5 = \boxed{}$

3. $5 \times \boxed{} = 35$

4. $\boxed{} \times 5 = 10$

5. $3 \times 5 = \boxed{}$

6. $50 / 5 = \boxed{}$

7. $5 \cdot 9 = \boxed{}$

8. $\boxed{} \cdot 5 = 20$

9. $5\overline{)25}$

10. $5 * \boxed{} = 40$

11. $5 \cdot 5 = \boxed{}$

12. $\dfrac{35}{5} = \boxed{}$

13. $5 \cdot \boxed{} = 15$

14. $30 \div 5 = \boxed{}$

15. $5 \times \boxed{} = 45$

16. $\boxed{} \div 5 = 7$

17. $\dfrac{10}{5} = \boxed{}$

18. $5 \cdot 8 = \boxed{}$

19. $5\overline{)20}$

20. $5 \times \boxed{} = 5$

21. $5 \times \boxed{} = 50$

12. 7 13. 3 14. 6 15. 9 16. 35 17. 2 18. 40 19. 4 20. 1 21. 10
1. 30 2. 9 3. 7 4. 2 5. 15 6. 10 7. 45 8. 4 9. 5 10. 8 11. 25

The Meaning of Division

Write a multiplication equation and a division equation for each problem. Then solve the problem.

1. Mandy's Diner has a total of 20 chairs. The chairs are divided equally among 5 tables. How many chairs are at each table?

   _____

2. Tarek divided 30 nickels into 5 piles. He put the same number of nickels in each pile. How many nickels were in each pile?

   _____

3. A group of singers has 45 members. The singers are arranged in groups of 5 on the stage. How many groups are there?

   _____

4. Brianna arranged 40 marbles into an array with 5 marbles in each row. How many rows of marbles were in her array?

   _____

Show your work.

Remembering

Solve each problem. If there is not enough information to solve the problem, tell what else you would need to know.

Show your work.

1. Mona wrote 7 serious poems and some funny poems. She wrote 12 poems in all. How many funny poems did she write?

_____

2. Lidia baked 14 cakes. She gave some cakes to her neighbors. How many cakes does Lidia have left?

_____

Use the bar graph to solve each problem.

3. How many more stuffed animals are there than bicycles?

_____

4. How many board games and stuffed animals are there altogether?

_____

5. How many fewer bicycles are there than board games?

_____

6. Write a problem using the information in the bar graph. Solve your problem.

_____

_____

_____

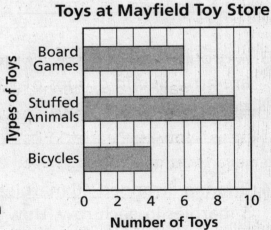

Toys at Mayfield Toy Store

The Meaning of Division

Name _____ **Date** _____

Homework

Use this chart to practice your 2s count-bys, multiplications, and divisions. Then have your Homework Helper test you.

	× In Order	× Mixed Up	÷ Mixed Up
2s	$1 \times 2 = 2$	$4 \times 2 = 8$	$18 \div 2 = 9$
	$2 \times 2 = 4$	$7 \times 2 = 14$	$6 \div 2 = 3$
	$3 \times 2 = 6$	$2 \times 2 = 4$	$2 \div 2 = 1$
	$4 \times 2 = 8$	$5 \times 2 = 10$	$16 \div 2 = 8$
	$5 \times 2 = 10$	$9 \times 2 = 18$	$14 \div 2 = 7$
	$6 \times 2 = 12$	$1 \times 2 = 2$	$4 \div 2 = 2$
	$7 \times 2 = 14$	$10 \times 2 = 20$	$20 \div 2 = 10$
	$8 \times 2 = 16$	$3 \times 2 = 6$	$8 \div 2 = 4$
	$9 \times 2 = 18$	$6 \times 2 = 12$	$12 \div 2 = 6$
	$10 \times 2 = 20$	$8 \times 2 = 16$	$10 \div 2 = 5$

Homework

Multiply or divide to find the unknown numbers. Then check your answers at the bottom of this page.

1. 2 × 4 = ☐   **2.** 20 ÷ 5 = ☐   **3.** 6 * 2 = ☐

4. 45 / 5 = ☐   **5.** 2 • 10 = ☐   **6.** $\frac{20}{2}$ = ☐

7. 5 × 10 = ☐   **8.** 16 ÷ 2 = ☐   **9.** 6 × 5 = ☐

10. 30 / 5 = ☐   **11.** 5 • 7 = ☐   **12.** 2)‾18

13. 8 * 2 = ☐   **14.** $\frac{25}{5}$ = ☐   **15.** 5 • 4 = ☐

16. 16 / 2 = ☐   **17.** 2)‾10   **18.** 2 * 7 = ☐

19. 5 × 5 = ☐   **20.** 14 ÷ 2 = ☐   **21.** $\frac{☐}{5}$ = 7

12. 9 13. 16 14. 5 15. 20 16. 8 17. 5 18. 14 19. 25 20. 7 21. 35
1. 8 2. 4 3. 12 4. 9 5. 20 6. 10 7. 50 8. 8 9. 30 10. 6 11. 35

Homework

Home Check Sheet 1: 5s and 2s

5s Multiplications	5s Divisions	2s Multiplications	2s Divisions
2 × 5 = 10	30 / 5 = 6	4 × 2 = 8	8 / 2 = 4
5 • 6 = 30	5 ÷ 5 = 1	2 • 8 = 16	18 ÷ 2 = 9
5 * 9 = 45	15 / 5 = 3	1 * 2 = 2	2 / 2 = 1
4 × 5 = 20	50 ÷ 5 = 10	6 × 2 = 12	16 ÷ 2 = 8
5 • 7 = 35	20 / 5 = 4	2 • 9 = 18	4 / 2 = 2
10 * 5 = 50	10 ÷ 5 = 2	2 * 2 = 4	20 ÷ 2 = 10
1 × 5 = 5	35 / 5 = 7	3 × 2 = 6	10 / 2 = 5
5 • 3 = 15	40 ÷ 5 = 8	2 • 5 = 10	12 ÷ 2 = 6
8 * 5 = 40	25 / 5 = 5	10 * 2 = 20	6 / 2 = 3
5 × 5 = 25	45 / 5 = 9	2 × 7 = 14	14 / 2 = 7
5 • 8 = 40	20 ÷ 5 = 4	2 • 10 = 20	4 ÷ 2 = 2
7 * 5 = 35	15 / 5 = 3	9 * 2 = 18	2 / 2 = 1
5 × 4 = 20	30 ÷ 5 = 6	2 × 6 = 12	8 ÷ 2 = 4
6 • 5 = 30	25 / 5 = 5	8 • 2 = 16	6 / 2 = 3
5 * 1 = 5	10 ÷ 5 = 2	2 * 3 = 6	20 ÷ 2 = 10
5 × 10 = 50	45 / 5 = 9	2 × 2 = 4	14 / 2 = 7
9 • 5 = 45	35 ÷ 5 = 7	1 • 2 = 2	10 ÷ 2 = 5
5 * 2 = 10	50 ÷ 5 = 10	2 * 4 = 8	16 ÷ 2 = 8
3 × 5 = 15	40 / 5 = 8	5 × 2 = 10	12 / 2 = 6
5 • 5 = 25	5 ÷ 5 = 1	7 • 2 = 14	18 ÷ 2 = 9

Homework

Study Plan

_____

Homework Helper

Solve each problem.

1. Tanya had 14 cups to fill with juice. She put them in 2 equal rows. How many cups were in each row?

_____

2. Rebecca has 3 pairs of running shoes. She bought new shoelaces for each pair. How many shoelaces did she buy?

_____

3. Jason served his family dinner. He put 5 carrots on each of the 4 plates. How many carrots did Jason serve in all?

_____

4. Olivia filled 8 vases with flowers. She put 5 flowers in each vase. How many flowers did she put in the vases?

_____

5. Devon has 30 model airplanes. He put the same number on each of the 5 shelves of his bookcase. How many model airplanes did Devon put on each shelf?

_____

6. There are 12 eggs in a carton. They are arranged in 2 rows with the same number of eggs in each row. How many eggs are in each row?

_____

Name _____ **Date** _____

Remembering

Find the missing numbers.

1. $9 + \boxed{} = 15$ **2.** $\boxed{} - 8 = 9$ **3.** $\boxed{} + 7 = 13$ **4.** $12 - \boxed{} = 7$

5. $\boxed{} + 8 = 11$ **6.** $13 - \boxed{} = 9$ **7.** $15 - \boxed{} = 9$ **8.** $7 + \boxed{} = 11$

Solve each problem. If there is not enough information to solve the problem, tell what else you would need to know.

Show your work.

9. On Saturday 324 people rode the Ferris wheel at the fair. Of these people, 126 rode during the morning. How many people rode during the rest of the day?

_____

10. Sam bought 3 new shirts and hung them in the closet with his other shirts. How many shirts does Sam have now?

_____

11. There are 20 notebooks on the store shelf. There are 6 yellow notebooks, and the rest are purple. Mark bought 2 purple notebooks. How many purple notebooks are left on the shelf?

_____

12. Tohmer had 13 pairs of clean socks. He wore some during the week. He has 5 pairs of clean socks left. How many pairs of socks did he wear this week?

_____

Round each money amount to the nearest dollar.

13. $9.72 _____ **14.** $4.87 _____ **15.** $6.39 _____

16. $12.20 _____ **17.** $7.67 _____ **18.** $3.43 _____

Multiply and Divide with 2

Name   **Date**

Homework

Use this chart to practice your 10s count-bys, multiplications, and divisions. Then have your Homework Helper test you.

	× In Order	× Mixed Up	÷ Mixed Up
10s	$1 \times 10 = 10$	$4 \times 10 = 40$	$100 \div 10 = 10$
	$2 \times 10 = 20$	$7 \times 10 = 70$	$20 \div 10 = 2$
	$3 \times 10 = 30$	$2 \times 10 = 20$	$40 \div 10 = 4$
	$4 \times 10 = 40$	$5 \times 10 = 50$	$70 \div 10 = 7$
	$5 \times 10 = 50$	$9 \times 10 = 90$	$30 \div 10 = 3$
	$6 \times 10 = 60$	$1 \times 10 = 10$	$60 \div 10 = 6$
	$7 \times 10 = 70$	$10 \times 10 = 100$	$80 \div 10 = 8$
	$8 \times 10 = 80$	$3 \times 10 = 30$	$10 \div 10 = 1$
	$9 \times 10 = 90$	$6 \times 10 = 60$	$50 \div 10 = 5$
	$10 \times 10 = 100$	$8 \times 10 = 80$	$90 \div 10 = 9$

Homework

Multiply or divide to find the unknown numbers. Then check your answers at the bottom of this page.

1. $2 \times 10 = \boxed{}$

2. $15 \div 5 = \boxed{}$

3. $4 * 2 = \boxed{}$

4. $80 / 10 = \boxed{}$

5. $5 \bullet \boxed{} = 40$

6. $\frac{60}{10} = \boxed{}$

7. $\boxed{} \times 5 = 30$

8. $\frac{24}{2} = \boxed{}$

9. $6 \times 10 = \boxed{}$

10. $25 / 5 = \boxed{}$

11. $10 \bullet 7 = \boxed{}$

12. $14 \div 2 = \boxed{}$

13. $9 * 2 = \boxed{}$

14. $\frac{45}{5} = \boxed{}$

15. $10 \bullet 4 = \boxed{}$

16. $2\overline{)20}$

17. $70 \div 10 = \boxed{}$

18. $9 * \boxed{} = 18$

19. $\boxed{} \times 5 = 35$

20. $\frac{\boxed{}}{3} = 10$

21. $\boxed{} \bullet 2 = 16$

1. 20 2. 3 3. 8 4. 8 5. 8 6. 6 7. 6 8. 12 9. 60 10. 5 11. 70 12. 7 13. 18 14. 9 15. 40 16. 10 17. 7 18. 2 19. 7 20. 30 21. 8

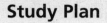

Study Plan

_____

Homework Helper

Solve each problem.

1. Wendy has $2.00. She wants to buy some marbles that cost $0.10 each. How many marbles can she buy?

   _____

2. Natalie turned off 2 lights in each of the 6 rooms of her house. How many lights did she turn off?

   _____

3. Luis has 18 single socks. How many pairs of socks does he have?

   _____

4. Lana has 9 nickels. She wants to buy an apple that cost $0.40. Does she have enough money?

   _____

5. Annabelle had 20 crayons. She gave 5 of them to each of her sisters. How many sisters does Annabelle have?

   _____

6. Harvey wrote letters to 10 of his friends. Each letter was 3 pages long. How many pages did Harvey write?

   _____

Complete the table.

7.

Number of Nickels	1	3	5	8	
Total Amount		15¢			45¢	50¢

Remembering

Vera had 163 marbles. Her older brother gave her his collection of 297 marbles. How many marbles does Vera have now?

1. Solve the problem. _____   *Show your work.*

2. Write a subtraction word problem related to the addition word problem. _____

   _____

   _____

   _____

3. Without doing any calculations, find the solution to the problem you wrote. _____

   _____

Jose spent $6.87 at the store. He spent $3.96 on markers and the rest on crayons. How much money did he spend on crayons?

4. Solve the problem. _____   *Show your work.*

5. Write an addition word problem related to the subtraction word problem.

   _____

   _____

   _____

6. Without doing any calculations, find the solution to the problem you wrote. _____

Use mental math to add or subtract.

7. $800 + 100 =$ _____   8. $540 - 20 =$ _____

9. $630 + 300 =$ _____   10. $300 - 150 =$ _____

Name

Date

Homework

Use this chart to practice your 9s count-bys, multiplications, and divisions. Then have your Homework Helper test you.

9s	× In Order	× Mixed Up	÷ Mixed Up
	$1 \times 9 = 9$	$4 \times 9 = 36$	$63 \div 9 = 7$
	$2 \times 9 = 18$	$7 \times 9 = 63$	$9 \div 9 = 1$
	$3 \times 9 = 27$	$2 \times 9 = 18$	$54 \div 9 = 6$
	$4 \times 9 = 36$	$5 \times 9 = 45$	$18 \div 9 = 2$
	$5 \times 9 = 45$	$9 \times 9 = 81$	$90 \div 9 = 10$
	$6 \times 9 = 54$	$1 \times 9 = 9$	$81 \div 9 = 9$
	$7 \times 9 = 63$	$10 \times 9 = 90$	$45 \div 9 = 5$
	$8 \times 9 = 72$	$3 \times 9 = 27$	$27 \div 9 = 3$
	$9 \times 9 = 81$	$6 \times 9 = 54$	$36 \div 9 = 4$
	$10 \times 9 = 90$	$8 \times 9 = 72$	$72 \div 9 = 8$

Homework

Multiply or divide to find the unknown numbers. Then check your answers at the bottom of this page.

1. $2 \times 9 = \boxed{}$

2. $18 \div 2 = \boxed{}$

3. $6 * \boxed{} = 12$

4. $40 / 5 = \boxed{}$

5. $10 \cdot 8 = \boxed{}$

6. $\dfrac{27}{9} = \boxed{}$

7. $\boxed{} \times 5 = 40$

8. $2\overline{)14}$ with box above

9. $9 \times 10 = \boxed{}$

10. $\dfrac{60}{10} = \boxed{}$

11. $10 \cdot 7 = \boxed{}$

12. $72 \div 9 = \boxed{}$

13. $2 * 9 = \boxed{}$

14. $\dfrac{20}{2} = \boxed{}$

15. $9 \cdot \boxed{} = 36$

16. $10 / 2 = \boxed{}$

17. $63 \div 9 = \boxed{}$

18. $9 * 9 = \boxed{}$

19. $5 \times 5 = \boxed{}$

20. $5\overline{)30}$ with box above

21. $9 \times 3 = \boxed{}$

1. 18 2. 9 3. 2 4. 8 5. 80 6. 3 7. 8 8. 7 9. 90 10. 6 11. 70
12. 8 13. 18 14. 10 15. 4 16. 5 17. 7 18. 81 19. 25 20. 6 21. 27

Multiply and Divide with 9

Name _____

Date _____

Home Check Sheet 2: 10s and 9s

10s Multiplications
9 × 10 = 90
10 • 3 = 30
10 * 6 = 60
1 × 10 = 10
10 • 4 = 40
10 * 7 = 70
8 × 10 = 80
10 • 10 = 100
5 * 10 = 50
10 × 2 = 20
10 • 5 = 50
4 * 10 = 40
10 × 1 = 10
3 • 10 = 30
10 * 8 = 80
7 × 10 = 70
6 • 10 = 60
10 * 9 = 90
10 × 10 = 100
2 • 10 = 20

10s Divisions
100 / 10 = 10
50 ÷ 10 = 5
70 / 10 = 7
40 ÷ 10 = 4
80 / 10 = 8
60 ÷ 10 = 6
10 / 10 = 1
20 ÷ 10 = 2
90 / 10 = 9
30 / 10 = 3
80 ÷ 10 = 8
70 / 10 = 7
100 ÷ 10 = 10
90 / 10 = 9
60 ÷ 10 = 6
30 / 10 = 3
10 ÷ 10 = 1
40 ÷ 10 = 4
20 / 10 = 2
50 ÷ 10 = 5

9s Multiplications
3 × 9 = 27
9 • 7 = 63
10 * 9 = 90
5 × 9 = 45
9 • 8 = 72
9 * 1 = 9
2 × 9 = 18
9 • 9 = 81
6 * 9 = 54
9 × 4 = 36
9 • 5 = 45
4 * 9 = 36
9 × 1 = 9
3 • 9 = 27
9 * 8 = 72
7 × 9 = 63
6 • 9 = 54
9 * 9 = 81
10 × 9 = 90
2 • 9 = 18

9s Divisions
27 / 9 = 3
9 ÷ 9 = 1
81 / 9 = 9
45 ÷ 9 = 5
90 / 9 = 10
36 ÷ 9 = 4
18 / 9 = 2
63 ÷ 9 = 7
54 / 9 = 6
72 / 9 = 8
27 ÷ 9 = 3
45 / 9 = 5
63 ÷ 9 = 7
72 / 9 = 8
54 ÷ 9 = 6
18 / 9 = 2
90 ÷ 9 = 10
9 ÷ 9 = 1
36 / 9 = 4
81 ÷ 9 = 9

Homework

Study Plan

Homework Helper

Write an equation for each situation. Then solve the problem.

Show your work.

1. The pet store has 54 birds. There are 9 birds in each cage. How many cages are there?

_____

2. George told 2 stories each night of the camping trip. The camping trip was 3 nights long. How many stories did George tell?

_____

3. LaShawna blew up 40 balloons for a party. She made 10 equal bunches of balloons to put on the tables. How many balloons were in each bunch?

_____

4. There are 4 floors in Redville City Hall. Every floor has 9 offices. How many offices are in the building?

_____

5. Brigitte has 15 CDs. She can put 5 CDs in the CD player at one time. How many times does she have to change the CDs to listen to all of them?

_____

Remembering

Round each number to the nearest hundred.

1. 359 _____   2. 642 _____   3. 121 _____

4. 298 _____   5. 971 _____   6. 750 _____

Round each number to the nearest ten.

7. 676 _____   8. 94 _____   9. 43 _____

10. 532 _____   11. 67 _____   12. 198 _____

Draw each figure if you can. If it is not possible, explain why.

13. a quadrilateral that is not a square

14. a parallelogram that is not a square

15. a rectangle that is not a parallelogram

16. a rectangle that is not a square

17. a square that is not a rectangle

18. a square that is not a parallelogram

Homework

Home Check Sheet 3: 2s, 5s, 9s, and 10s

2s, 5s, 9s, 10s Multiplications	2s, 5s, 9s, 10s Multiplications	2s, 5s, 9s, 10s Divisions	2s, 5s, 9s, 10s Divisions
$2 \times 10 = 20$	$5 \times 10 = 50$	$18 / 2 = 9$	$36 / 9 = 4$
$10 \cdot 5 = 50$	$10 \cdot 9 = 90$	$50 \div 5 = 10$	$70 \div 10 = 7$
$9 * 6 = 54$	$4 * 10 = 40$	$72 / 9 = 8$	$18 / 2 = 9$
$7 \times 10 = 70$	$2 \times 9 = 18$	$60 \div 10 = 6$	$45 \div 5 = 9$
$2 \cdot 3 = 6$	$5 \cdot 3 = 15$	$12 / 2 = 6$	$45 \div 9 = 5$
$5 * 7 = 35$	$6 * 9 = 54$	$30 \div 5 = 6$	$30 \div 10 = 3$
$9 \times 10 = 90$	$10 \times 3 = 30$	$18 / 9 = 2$	$6 / 2 = 3$
$6 \cdot 10 = 60$	$3 \cdot 2 = 6$	$50 \div 10 = 5$	$50 \div 5 = 10$
$8 * 2 = 16$	$5 * 8 = 40$	$14 / 2 = 7$	$27 / 9 = 3$
$5 \times 6 = 30$	$9 \times 9 = 81$	$25 / 5 = 5$	$70 / 10 = 7$
$9 \cdot 5 = 45$	$10 \cdot 4 = 40$	$81 \div 9 = 9$	$20 \div 2 = 10$
$8 * 10 = 80$	$9 * 2 = 18$	$20 / 10 = 2$	$45 / 5 = 9$
$2 \times 1 = 2$	$5 \times 1 = 5$	$8 \div 2 = 4$	$54 \div 9 = 6$
$3 \cdot 5 = 15$	$9 \cdot 6 = 54$	$45 / 5 = 9$	$80 / 10 = 8$
$4 * 9 = 36$	$10 * 1 = 10$	$63 \div 9 = 7$	$16 \div 2 = 8$
$3 \times 10 = 30$	$7 \times 2 = 14$	$30 / 10 = 3$	$15 / 5 = 3$
$2 \cdot 6 = 12$	$6 \cdot 5 = 30$	$10 \div 2 = 5$	$90 \div 9 = 10$
$4 * 5 = 20$	$8 * 9 = 72$	$40 \div 5 = 8$	$100 \div 10 = 10$
$9 \times 7 = 63$	$10 \times 6 = 60$	$9 / 9 = 1$	$12 / 2 = 6$
$1 \cdot 10 = 10$	$2 \cdot 8 = 16$	$50 \div 10 = 5$	$35 \div 5 = 7$

Name _____ Date _____

Homework

Multiply or divide to find the unknown numbers. Then check your answers at the bottom of this page.

1. $5 \times 6 = \boxed{}$

2. $50 \div 10 = \boxed{}$

3. $6 * 9 = \boxed{}$

4. $12 / 2 = \boxed{}$

5. $9 \times \boxed{} = 72$

6. $\dfrac{14}{2} = \boxed{}$

7. $9 \cdot 5 = \boxed{}$

8. $15 \div 5 = \boxed{}$

9. $7 \times 2 = \boxed{}$

10. $25 / 5 = \boxed{}$

11. $10 \cdot \boxed{} = 40$

12. $9\overline{)27}$

13. $8 * 5 = \boxed{}$

14. $\dfrac{81}{9} = \boxed{}$

15. $7 \cdot \boxed{} = 35$

16. $2\overline{)20}$

17. $10 \div \boxed{} = 5$

18. $2 * 7 = \boxed{}$

19. $30 \div 5 = \boxed{}$

20. $2 \times 7 = \boxed{}$

21. $18 / 2 = \boxed{}$

1. 30 2. 5 3. 54 4. 6 5. 8 6. 7 7. 45 8. 3 9. 14 10. 5 11. 4 12. 3 13. 40 14. 9 15. 5 16. 10 17. 2 18. 14 19. 6 20. 14 21. 9

Fluency Day for 2s, 5s, 9s, and 10s

Name _____ **Date** _____

Homework

```
┌─────────────────────────────────────────────────────────────┐
│ Study Plan                                                    │
│                                                               │
│                                                               │
│                                    _____    │
│                                         Homework Helper       │
└─────────────────────────────────────────────────────────────┘
```

Write an equation for each situation. Then solve the problem.

1. Quinn rode his bike 35 miles. He stopped for water every 5 miles. How many times did Quinn stop for water?

_____

2. Roy had 12 bottles of juice. He put them in the refrigerator in 2 rows. How many bottles were in each row?

_____

3. Melinda has 5 cousins. She called each one on the phone 4 times this month. How many phone calls did she make to her cousins this month?

_____

4. Janelle won 27 tickets at the fair. She traded the tickets for 9 prizes. Each prize was worth the same number of tickets. How many tickets were each prize worth?

_____

5. Eric had 2 picnic baskets. He put 7 apples in each one. How many apples did he put into the picnic baskets?

_____

6. Grace has read 2 chapters in each of her 9 books. How many chapters has she read in all?

_____

Remembering

Solve each problem.

Show your work.

1. Jake had 16 model planes. He gave 4 of them to his brother. How many model planes did Jake have left?

_____

2. Ahmed and Tray are playing air hockey. Ahmed has made 10 goals. He has made 3 more goals than Tray. How many goals has Tray made?

_____

3. There are 875 students at Prairie Hill School. Of these students, 467 are in the elementary school. The rest are in junior high. How many students are in junior high?

_____

Use the bar graph to solve each problem.

4. How much money was earned altogether from the sale of artwork and trips?

_____

5. How much more money was earned from the sale of artwork than furniture?

_____

6. Write a problem using the information in the bar graph. Solve your problem.

_____

_____

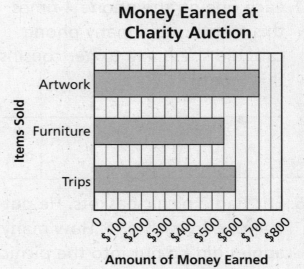

Money Earned at Charity Auction

Items Sold: Artwork, Furniture, Trips

Amount of Money Earned: $0 $100 $200 $300 $400 $500 $600 $700 $800

Homework

Use this chart to practice your 3s count-bys, multiplications, and divisions. Then have your Homework Helper test you.

3s	× In Order	× Mixed Up	÷ Mixed Up
	$1 \times 3 = 3$	$3 \times 3 = 9$	$27 \div 3 = 9$
	$2 \times 3 = 6$	$5 \times 3 = 15$	$21 \div 3 = 7$
	$3 \times 3 = 9$	$1 \times 3 = 3$	$3 \div 3 = 1$
	$4 \times 3 = 12$	$8 \times 3 = 24$	$9 \div 3 = 3$
	$5 \times 3 = 15$	$2 \times 3 = 6$	$30 \div 3 = 10$
	$6 \times 3 = 18$	$9 \times 3 = 27$	$24 \div 3 = 8$
	$7 \times 3 = 21$	$7 \times 3 = 21$	$12 \div 3 = 4$
	$8 \times 3 = 24$	$10 \times 3 = 30$	$6 \div 3 = 2$
	$9 \times 3 = 27$	$6 \times 3 = 18$	$15 \div 3 = 5$
	$10 \times 3 = 30$	$4 \times 3 = 12$	$18 \div 3 = 6$

Homework

Multiply or divide to find the unknown numbers. Then check your answers at the bottom of this page.

1. $6 \times 3 = \boxed{}$

2. $3\overline{)27}$ with $\boxed{}$ above

3. $2 * \boxed{} = 18$

4. $18 / 9 = \boxed{}$

5. $3 \times \boxed{} = 30$

6. $\dfrac{15}{3} = \boxed{}$

7. $9 \cdot 8 = \boxed{}$

8. $50 \div 10 = \boxed{}$

9. $2 \times 2 = \boxed{}$

10. $35 / 5 = \boxed{}$

11. $4 \cdot 10 = \boxed{}$

12. $14 \div 2 = \boxed{}$

13. $8 * 3 = \boxed{}$

14. $\dfrac{63}{9} = \boxed{}$

15. $5 \cdot \boxed{} = 35$

16. $9\overline{)27}$ with $\boxed{}$ above

17. $10 \div \boxed{} = 2$

18. $\boxed{} * 9 = 18$

19. $5 \times 9 = \boxed{}$

20. $81 \div \boxed{} = 9$

21. $14 / 2 = \boxed{}$

1. 18 2. 9 3. 9 4. 2 5. 10 6. 5 7. 72 8. 5 9. 4 10. 7 11. 40
12. 7 13. 24 14. 7 15. 7 16. 3 17. 5 18. 2 19. 45 20. 9 21. 7

Multiply and Divide with 3

Homework

Study Plan

_____

Homework Helper

Solve each problem.

1. Greg has 3 hats. He has worn each one 4 times this year. How many times this year has he worn a hat?

_____

2. Keenan has won 24 award ribbons. He hung them on his wall in 3 rows, with the same number of ribbons in each row. How many ribbons are in each row?

_____

3. Mai went to the movies 9 times this month. She paid 4 dollars to see each movie. How much did she spend in all?

_____

4. Tess planted 45 tomato seeds in her garden. She planted them in an array with 9 rows. How many seeds were in each row?

_____

Find the total number by starting with the fifth count-by and counting from there.

5. How many bananas are in these 9 bunches?

___ ___ ___ ___

Name _____

Date _____

Remembering

Write the total amount of money.

1.

_____

2.

_____

Solve each problem.

3. Miki's Ice Cream Parlor sold 345 scoops of ice cream on Saturday and 21 scoops on Sunday. How many more scoops were sold on Saturday than on Sunday?

_____

4. Terry went for a drive and used 5 gallons of gas. There are 6 gallons of gas left in his car. How many gallons were in Terry's car before his drive?

_____

5. Steven took 10 photographs of animals and 13 photographs of flowers. Then he took 6 more photographs of animals. How many photographs of animals did Steven take?

_____

6. Tia has 5 pancakes on her plate. Colin has 9 pancakes on his plate. How many more pancakes does Colin have than Tia?

_____

Multiply and Divide with 3

2×2

$\begin{array}{r} 2 \\ \times\ 3 \end{array}$ $\begin{array}{r} 3 \\ \times\ 2 \end{array}$

2×4
4×2

$\begin{array}{r} 2 \\ \times\ 5 \end{array}$ $\begin{array}{r} 5 \\ \times\ 2 \end{array}$

2×6
6×2

$\begin{array}{r} 2 \\ \times\ 7 \end{array}$ $\begin{array}{r} 7 \\ \times\ 2 \end{array}$

2×8
8×2

$\begin{array}{r} 2 \\ \times\ 9 \end{array}$ $\begin{array}{r} 9 \\ \times\ 2 \end{array}$

Card 1

$10 = 2 \times 5$
$10 = 5 \times 2$

5	2
10	4
	6
	8
	10

5
2 ○○○○○ 10

Card 2

$$\begin{array}{r} 2 \\ \times\, 4 \\ \hline 8 \end{array} \qquad \begin{array}{r} 4 \\ \times\, 2 \\ \hline 8 \end{array}$$

2 / 4 / 6 / 8   4 / 8

2
4 ○ 8

Card 3

$6 = 2 \times 3$
$6 = 3 \times 2$

3	2
6	4
	6

3
2 ○○ 6

Card 4

$$\begin{array}{r} 2 \\ \times\, 2 \\ \hline 4 \end{array}$$

2 / 4

2
2 ○ 4

Card 5

$18 = 2 \times 9$
$18 = 9 \times 2$

9	2
18	4
	6
	8
	10
	12
	14
	16
	18

9
2 ○○○○○○○○○ 18

Card 6

$$\begin{array}{r} 2 \\ \times\, 8 \\ \hline 16 \end{array} \qquad \begin{array}{r} 8 \\ \times\, 2 \\ \hline 16 \end{array}$$

8 / 16   2 / 4 / 6 / 8 / 10 / 12 / 14 / 16

2
8 16

Card 7

$14 = 2 \times 7$
$14 = 7 \times 2$

7	2
14	4
	6
	8
	10
	12
	14

7
2 ○○○○○○○ 14

Card 8

$$\begin{array}{r} 2 \\ \times\, 6 \\ \hline 12 \end{array} \qquad \begin{array}{r} 6 \\ \times\, 2 \\ \hline 12 \end{array}$$

6 / 12   2 / 4 / 6 / 8 / 10 / 12

2
6 12

Home Multiplication Strategy Cards

3×3

$$\begin{array}{r} 3 \\ \times\, 4 \\ \hline \end{array} \qquad \begin{array}{r} 4 \\ \times\, 3 \\ \hline \end{array}$$

3×5
5×3

$$\begin{array}{r} 3 \\ \times\, 6 \\ \hline \end{array} \qquad \begin{array}{r} 6 \\ \times\, 3 \\ \hline \end{array}$$

3×7
7×3

$$\begin{array}{r} 3 \\ \times\, 8 \\ \hline \end{array} \qquad \begin{array}{r} 8 \\ \times\, 3 \\ \hline \end{array}$$

3×9
9×3

$$\begin{array}{r} 4 \\ \times\, 4 \\ \hline \end{array}$$

$$18 = 3 \times 6$$
$$18 = 6 \times 3$$

6	3
12	6
18	9
	12
	15
	18

6
3 ○ 18

$$\begin{array}{c} 3 \\ \times 5 \\ \hline 15 \end{array} \qquad \begin{array}{c} 5 \\ \times 3 \\ \hline 15 \end{array}$$

5	3
10	6
15	9
	12
	15

3
5 ○ 15

$$12 = 3 \times 4$$
$$12 = 4 \times 3$$

4	3
8	6
12	9
	12

4
3 ○ 12

$$\begin{array}{c} 3 \\ \times 3 \\ \hline 9 \end{array}$$

3
6
9

3
3 ○ 9

$$16 = 4 \times 4$$

4
8
12
16

4
4 ○ 16

$$\begin{array}{c} 3 \\ \times 9 \\ \hline 27 \end{array} \qquad \begin{array}{c} 9 \\ \times 3 \\ \hline 27 \end{array}$$

9	3
18	6
27	9
	12
	15
	18
	21
	24
	27

9
3 ○ 27

$$24 = 3 \times 8$$
$$24 = 8 \times 3$$

8	3
16	6
24	9
	12
	15
	18
	21
	24

3
8 ○ 24

$$\begin{array}{c} 3 \\ \times 7 \\ \hline 21 \end{array} \qquad \begin{array}{c} 7 \\ \times 3 \\ \hline 21 \end{array}$$

7	3
14	6
21	9
	12
	15
	18
	21

7
3 ○ 21

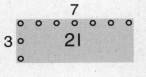

Home Multiplication Strategy Cards

4×5
5×4

$$\begin{array}{r} 4 \\ \times\ 6 \\ \hline \end{array} \qquad \begin{array}{r} 6 \\ \times\ 4 \\ \hline \end{array}$$

4×7
7×4

$$\begin{array}{r} 4 \\ \times\ 8 \\ \hline \end{array} \qquad \begin{array}{r} 8 \\ \times\ 4 \\ \hline \end{array}$$

4×9
9×4

$$\begin{array}{r} 5 \\ \times\ 5 \\ \hline \end{array}$$

5×6
6×5

$$\begin{array}{r} 5 \\ \times\ 7 \\ \hline \end{array} \qquad \begin{array}{r} 7 \\ \times\ 5 \\ \hline \end{array}$$

32 = 4 × 8
32 = 8 × 4

8	4
16	8
24	12
32	16
	20
	24
	28
	32

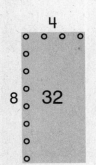

4   7
× 7   × 4
28   28

7	4
14	8
21	12
28	16
	20
	24
	28

24 = 4 × 6
24 = 6 × 4

6	4
12	8
18	12
24	16
	20
	24

4   5
× 5   × 4
20   20

5	4
10	8
15	12
20	16
	20

35 = 5 × 7
35 = 7 × 5

7	5
14	10
21	15
28	20
35	25
	30
	35

5   6
× 6   × 5
30   30

6	5
12	10
18	15
24	20
30	25
	30

25 = 5 × 5

5
10
15
20
25

4   9
× 9   × 4
36   36

9	4
18	8
27	12
36	16
	20
	24
	28
	32
	36

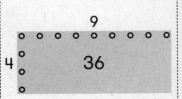

Home Multiplication Strategy Cards

5 × 8
8 × 5

$$\begin{array}{r} 5 \\ \times\ 9 \\ \hline \end{array} \qquad \begin{array}{r} 9 \\ \times\ 5 \\ \hline \end{array}$$

6 × 6

$$\begin{array}{r} 6 \\ \times\ 7 \\ \hline \end{array} \qquad \begin{array}{r} 7 \\ \times\ 6 \\ \hline \end{array}$$

6 × 8
8 × 6

$$\begin{array}{r} 6 \\ \times\ 9 \\ \hline \end{array} \qquad \begin{array}{r} 9 \\ \times\ 6 \\ \hline \end{array}$$

7 × 7

$$\begin{array}{r} 7 \\ \times\ 8 \\ \hline \end{array} \qquad \begin{array}{r} 8 \\ \times\ 7 \\ \hline \end{array}$$

$42 = 7 \times 6$ $42 = 6 \times 7$	$\begin{array}{r} 6 \\ \times\,6 \\ \hline 36 \end{array}$	$45 = 9 \times 5$ $45 = 5 \times 9$	$\begin{array}{r} 8 \\ \times\,5 \\ \hline 40 \end{array}$ $\quad$ $\begin{array}{r} 5 \\ \times\,8 \\ \hline 40 \end{array}$

Card 1

6	7
12	14
18	21
24	28
30	35
36	42
42	

7 × 6 = 42

Card 2

6
12
18
24
30

36

6 × 6 = 36

Card 3

5	9
10	18
15	27
20	36
25	45
30	
35	
40	
45	

9 × 5 = 45

Card 4

5	8
10	16
15	24
20	32
25	40
30	
35	
40	

5 × 8 = 40

$56 = 7 \times 8$ $56 = 8 \times 7$	$\begin{array}{r} 7 \\ \times\,7 \\ \hline 49 \end{array}$	$54 = 9 \times 6$ $54 = 6 \times 9$	$\begin{array}{r} 6 \\ \times\,8 \\ \hline 48 \end{array}$ $\quad$ $\begin{array}{r} 8 \\ \times\,6 \\ \hline 48 \end{array}$

Card 5

8	7
16	14
24	21
32	28
40	35
48	42
56	49
	56

7 × 8 = 56

Card 6

7
14
21
28
35

42
49

7 × 7 = 49

Card 7

6	9
12	18
18	27
24	36
30	45
36	54
42	
48	
54	

9 × 6 = 54

Card 8

6	8
12	16
18	24
24	32
30	40
36	48
42	
48	

8 × 6 = 48

Home Multiplication Strategy Cards

7×9
9×7

$$\begin{array}{r} 8 \\ \times\ 8 \\ \hline \end{array}$$

9×8
8×9

$$\begin{array}{r} 9 \\ \times\ 9 \\ \hline \end{array}$$

Card 1

$81 = 9 \times 9$

9
18
27
36
45

54
63
72
81

9

9 | 81

Card 2

$\begin{array}{r} 9 \\ \times 8 \\ \hline 72 \end{array}$ $\begin{array}{r} 8 \\ \times 9 \\ \hline 72 \end{array}$

8   9
16   18
24   27
32   36
40   45

48   54
56   63
64   72
72

9

8 | 72

Card 3

$64 = 8 \times 8$

8
16
24
32
40

48
56
64

8

8 | 64

Card 4

$\begin{array}{r} 7 \\ \times 9 \\ \hline 63 \end{array}$ $\begin{array}{r} 9 \\ \times 7 \\ \hline 63 \end{array}$

9   7
18   14
27   21
36   28
45   35

54   42
63   49
     56
     63

9

7 | 63

Home Multiplication Strategy Cards

$2\overline{)4}$	$2\overline{)6}$	$2\overline{)8}$	$2\overline{)10}$
$4 \div 2$	$6 \div 2$	$8 \div 2$	$10 \div 2$

$2\overline{)12}$	$2\overline{)14}$	$2\overline{)16}$	$2\overline{)18}$
$12 \div 2$	$14 \div 2$	$16 \div 2$	$18 \div 2$

5 2	4 2	3 2	2
$2\overline{)10}$ $5\overline{)10}$	$2\overline{)8}$ $4\overline{)8}$	$2\overline{)6}$ $3\overline{)6}$	$2\overline{)4}$

Card 1: 2, 4, 6, 8, 10 — 5, 10

Card 2: 2, 4, 6, 8 — 4, 8

Card 3: 2, 4, 6 — 3, 6

Card 4: 2, 4

5 — 2 : 10
4 — 2 : 8
3 — 2 : 6
2 — 2 : 4

9 2	8 2	7 2	6 2
$2\overline{)18}$ $9\overline{)18}$	$2\overline{)16}$ $8\overline{)16}$	$2\overline{)14}$ $7\overline{)14}$	$2\overline{)12}$ $6\overline{)12}$

Card 5: 2, 4, 6, 8, 10, 12, 14, 16, 18 — 9, 18

Card 6: 2, 4, 6, 8, 10, 12, 14, 16 — 8, 16

Card 7: 2, 4, 6, 8, 10, 12, 14 — 7, 14

Card 8: 2, 4, 6, 8, 10, 12 — 6, 12

9 — 2 : 18
8 — 2 : 16
7 — 2 : 14
6 — 2 : 12

Home Division Strategy Cards

$$3\overline{)6}$$
$$6 \div 3$$

$$4\overline{)8}$$
$$8 \div 4$$

$$5\overline{)10}$$
$$10 \div 5$$

$$6\overline{)12}$$
$$12 \div 6$$

$$7\overline{)14}$$
$$14 \div 7$$

$$8\overline{)16}$$
$$16 \div 8$$

$$9\overline{)18}$$
$$18 \div 9$$

$$3\overline{)9}$$
$$9 \div 3$$

$$\begin{array}{c}2\\6\overline{)12}\end{array}\qquad\begin{array}{c}6\\2\overline{)12}\end{array}$$

6
12

2
4
6
8
10

12

$$\begin{array}{c}2\\5\overline{)10}\end{array}\qquad\begin{array}{c}5\\2\overline{)10}\end{array}$$

5
10

2
4
6
8
10

$$\begin{array}{c}2\\4\overline{)8}\end{array}\qquad\begin{array}{c}4\\2\overline{)8}\end{array}$$

4
8

2
4
6
8

$$\begin{array}{c}2\\3\overline{)6}\end{array}\qquad\begin{array}{c}3\\2\overline{)6}\end{array}$$

3
6

2
4
6

$$\begin{array}{c}3\\3\overline{)9}\end{array}$$

3
6
9

$$\begin{array}{c}2\\9\overline{)18}\end{array}\qquad\begin{array}{c}9\\2\overline{)18}\end{array}$$

9
18

2
4
6
8
10

12
14
16
18

$$\begin{array}{c}2\\8\overline{)16}\end{array}\qquad\begin{array}{c}8\\2\overline{)16}\end{array}$$

8
16

2
4
6
8
10

12
14
16

$$\begin{array}{c}2\\7\overline{)14}\end{array}\qquad\begin{array}{c}7\\2\overline{)14}\end{array}$$

7
14

2
4
6
8
10

12
14

Home Division Strategy Cards

$3\overline{)12}$

$12 \div 3$

$3\overline{)15}$

$15 \div 3$

$3\overline{)18}$

$18 \div 3$

$3\overline{)21}$

$21 \div 3$

$3\overline{)24}$

$24 \div 3$

$3\overline{)27}$

$27 \div 3$

$4\overline{)12}$

$12 \div 4$

$5\overline{)15}$

$15 \div 5$

7   **3**

3)21   7)21

3   7
6   14
9   21
12
15

18
21

7
3 21

3   **6**

3)18   6)18

3   6
6   12
9   18
12
15

18

6
3 18

5   **3**

3)15   5)15

3   5
6   10
9   15
12
15

5
3 15

4   **3**

3)12   4)12

3   4
6   8
9   12
12

4
3 12

---

3   **5**

5)15   3)15

5   3
10   6
15   9
         12
         15

3
5 15

3   **4**

4)12   3)12

4   3
8   6
12   9
         12

3
4 12

9   **3**

3)27   9)27

3   9
6   18
9   27
12
15

18
21
24
27

9
3 27

8   **3**

3)24   8)24

3   8
6   16
9   24
12
15

18
21
24

8
3 24

Home Division Strategy Cards

$6\overline{)18}$

$18 \div 6$

$7\overline{)21}$

$21 \div 7$

$8\overline{)24}$

$24 \div 8$

$9\overline{)27}$

$27 \div 9$

$4\overline{)16}$

$16 \div 4$

$4\overline{)20}$

$20 \div 4$

$4\overline{)24}$

$24 \div 4$

$4\overline{)28}$

$28 \div 4$

Home Division Strategy Cards

3
9)27
9
18
27

9
3)27
3
6
9
12
15

18
21
24
27

Array: 3 × 9 = 27

3
8)24
8
16
24

8
3)24
3
6
9
12
15

18
21
24

Array: 3 × 8 = 24

3
7)21
7
14
21

7
3)21
3
6
9
12
15

18
21

Array: 3 × 7 = 21

3
6)18
6
12
18

6
3)18
3
6
9
12
15
18

Array: 3 × 6 = 18

7
4)28
4
8
12
16
20

24
28

4
7)28
7
14
21
28

Array: 7 × 4 = 28

6
4)24
4
8
12
16
20

24

4
6)24
6
12
18
24

Array: 6 × 4 = 24

5
4)20
4
8
12
16
20

4
5)20
5
10
15
20

Array: 5 × 4 = 20

4
4)16
4
8
12
16

Array: 4 × 4 = 16

Home Division Strategy Cards

$4\overline{)32}$

$32 \div 4$

$4\overline{)36}$

$36 \div 4$

$5\overline{)20}$

$20 \div 5$

$6\overline{)24}$

$24 \div 6$

$7\overline{)28}$

$28 \div 7$

$8\overline{)32}$

$32 \div 8$

$9\overline{)36}$

$36 \div 9$

$5\overline{)25}$

$25 \div 5$

$$4 \overline{)6)24} \quad 6 \overline{)4)24}$$

6   4
12   8
18 12
24 16
    20
    24

4
6 | 24

$$4 \overline{)5)20} \quad 5 \overline{)4)20}$$

5   4
10 8
15 12
20 16
    20

4
20

$$9 \overline{)4)36} \quad 4 \overline{)9)36}$$

4   9
8   18
12 27
16 36
20
24
28
32
36

9
36

$$8 \overline{)4)32} \quad 4 \overline{)8)32}$$

4   8
8 16
12 24
16 32
20
24
28
32

8
32

$$5 \overline{)5)25}$$

5
10
15
20
25

5
5 | 25

$$4 \overline{)9)36} \quad 9 \overline{)4)36}$$

9   4
18 8
27 12
36 16
    20
    24
    28
    32
    36

4
9 | 36

$$4 \overline{)8)32} \quad 8 \overline{)4)32}$$

8   4
16 8
24 12
32 16
    20
    24
    28
    32

4
8 | 32

$$4 \overline{)7)28} \quad 7 \overline{)4)28}$$

7   4
14 8
21 12
28 16
    20
    24
    28

4
7 | 28

Home Division Strategy Cards

$5 \overline{)30}$

$30 \div 5$

$5 \overline{)35}$

$35 \div 5$

$5 \overline{)40}$

$40 \div 5$

$5 \overline{)45}$

$45 \div 5$

$6 \overline{)30}$

$30 \div 6$

$7 \overline{)35}$

$35 \div 7$

$8 \overline{)40}$

$40 \div 8$

$9 \overline{)45}$

$45 \div 9$

Home Division Strategy Cards

$6\overline{)36}$

$36 \div 6$

$6\overline{)42}$

$42 \div 6$

$6\overline{)48}$

$48 \div 6$

$6\overline{)54}$

$54 \div 6$

$7\overline{)42}$

$42 \div 7$

$8\overline{)48}$

$48 \div 8$

$9\overline{)54}$

$54 \div 9$

$7\overline{)49}$

$49 \div 7$

Home Division Strategy Cards **173**

9
6)54 **6**
9)54

6
12
18
24
30

36
42
48
54

9
18
27
36
45

54

9
6 | 54

8
6)48 **6**
8)48

6
12
18
24
30

36
42
48

8
16
24
32
40

48

8
6 | 48

7
6)42 **6**
7)42

6
12
18
24
30

36
42

7
14
21
28
35

42

7
6 | 42

6
6)36

6
12
18
24
30

36

6
6 | 36

7
7)49

7
14
21
28
35

42
49

7
7 | 49

6
9)54 **9**
6)54

9
18
27
36
45

54

6
12
18
24
30

36
42
48
54

6
9 | 54

6
8)48 **8**
6)48

8
16
24
32
40

48

6
12
18
24
30

36
42
48

6
8 | 48

6
7)42 **7**
6)42

7
14
21
28
35

42

6
12
18
24
30

36
42

6
7 | 42

$7\overline{)56}$

$56 \div 7$

$7\overline{)63}$

$63 \div 7$

$8\overline{)56}$

$56 \div 8$

$9\overline{)63}$

$63 \div 9$

$8\overline{)64}$

$64 \div 8$

$8\overline{)72}$

$72 \div 8$

$9\overline{)72}$

$72 \div 9$

$9\overline{)81}$

$81 \div 9$

7   **9**
9)63 7)63

9	7
18	14
27	21
36	28
45	35
54	42
63	49
	56
	63

7
9 63

7   **8**
8)56 7)56

8	7
16	14
24	21
32	28
40	35
48	42
56	49
	56

7
8 56

9   **7**
7)63 9)63

7	9
14	18
21	27
28	36
35	45
42	54
49	63
56	
63	

9
7 63

8   **7**
7)56 8)56

7	8
14	16
21	24
28	32
35	40
42	48
49	56
56	

8
7 56

9
9)81

9
18
27
36
45
54
63
72
81

9
9 81

8   **9**
9)72 8)72

9	8
18	16
27	24
36	32
45	40
54	48
63	56
72	64
	72

8
9 72

9   **8**
8)72 9)72

8	9
16	18
24	27
32	36
40	45
48	54
56	63
64	72
72	

9
8 72

8
8)64

8
16
24
32
40
48
56
64

8
8 64

Home Division Strategy Cards

Homework

Home Study Sheet B

3s

Count-bys	Mixed Up ×	Mixed Up ÷
1 × 3 = 3	5 × 3 = 15	27 ÷ 3 = 9
2 × 3 = 6	1 × 3 = 3	6 ÷ 3 = 2
3 × 3 = 9	8 × 3 = 24	18 ÷ 3 = 6
4 × 3 = 12	10 × 3 = 30	30 ÷ 3 = 10
5 × 3 = 15	3 × 3 = 9	9 ÷ 3 = 3
6 × 3 = 18	7 × 3 = 21	3 ÷ 3 = 1
7 × 3 = 21	9 × 3 = 27	12 ÷ 3 = 4
8 × 3 = 24	2 × 3 = 6	24 ÷ 3 = 8
9 × 3 = 27	4 × 3 = 12	15 ÷ 3 = 5
10 × 3 = 30	6 × 3 = 18	21 ÷ 3 = 7

4s

Count-bys	Mixed Up ×	Mixed Up ÷
1 × 4 = 4	4 × 4 = 16	12 ÷ 4 = 3
2 × 4 = 8	1 × 4 = 4	36 ÷ 4 = 9
3 × 4 = 12	7 × 4 = 28	24 ÷ 4 = 6
4 × 4 = 16	3 × 4 = 12	4 ÷ 4 = 1
5 × 4 = 20	9 × 4 = 36	20 ÷ 4 = 5
6 × 4 = 24	10 × 4 = 40	28 ÷ 4 = 7
7 × 4 = 28	2 × 4 = 8	8 ÷ 4 = 2
8 × 4 = 32	5 × 4 = 20	40 ÷ 4 = 10
9 × 4 = 36	8 × 4 = 32	32 ÷ 4 = 8
10 × 4 = 40	6 × 4 = 24	16 ÷ 4 = 4

1s

Count-bys	Mixed Up ×	Mixed Up ÷
1 × 1 = 1	5 × 1 = 5	10 ÷ 1 = 10
2 × 1 = 2	7 × 1 = 7	8 ÷ 1 = 8
3 × 1 = 3	10 × 1 = 10	4 ÷ 1 = 4
4 × 1 = 4	1 × 1 = 1	9 ÷ 1 = 9
5 × 1 = 5	8 × 1 = 8	6 ÷ 1 = 6
6 × 1 = 6	4 × 1 = 4	7 ÷ 1 = 7
7 × 1 = 7	9 × 1 = 9	1 ÷ 1 = 1
8 × 1 = 8	3 × 1 = 3	2 ÷ 1 = 2
9 × 1 = 9	2 × 1 = 2	5 ÷ 1 = 5
10 × 1 = 10	6 × 1 = 6	3 ÷ 1 = 3

0s

Count-bys	Mixed Up ×
1 × 0 = 0	3 × 0 = 0
2 × 0 = 0	10 × 0 = 0
3 × 0 = 0	5 × 0 = 0
4 × 0 = 0	8 × 0 = 0
5 × 0 = 0	7 × 0 = 0
6 × 0 = 0	2 × 0 = 0
7 × 0 = 0	9 × 0 = 0
8 × 0 = 0	6 × 0 = 0
9 × 0 = 0	1 × 0 = 0
10 × 0 = 0	4 × 0 = 0

Name _____ **Date** _____

Homework

Multiply or divide to find the unknown numbers. Then check your answers at the bottom of the page.

1. $3 \times 5 =$ ☐

2. $27 \div 9 =$ ☐

3. $2\overline{)20}$ ☐

4. $7 \bullet 9 =$ ☐

5. $2 *$ ☐ $= 12$

6. $18 / 3 =$ ☐

7. $9 \times 5 =$ ☐

8. $3 *$ ☐ $= 21$

9. $\dfrac{81}{9} =$ ☐

10. $6 \div 3 =$ ☐

11. $8 \times 2 =$ ☐

12. $\dfrac{14}{2} =$ ☐

13. $3 \bullet 3 =$ ☐

14. ☐ $* 9 = 72$

15. $90 \div 9 =$ ☐

16. ☐ $* 2 = 18$

17. $24 \div$ ☐ $= 8$

18. $12 /$ ☐ $= 6$

19. $6 \bullet 5 =$ ☐

20. $4 \times$ ☐ $= 40$

21. ☐ $\bullet 9 = 54$

1. 15 **2.** 3 **3.** 10 **4.** 63 **5.** 6 **6.** 6 **7.** 45 **8.** 7 **9.** 9 **10.** 2 **11.** 16
12. 7 **13.** 9 **14.** 8 **15.** 10 **16.** 9 **17.** 3 **18.** 2 **19.** 30 **20.** 10 **21.** 6

Multiplication and Area

Name _____ **Date** _____

Homework

**Make a rectangle drawing to represent each exercise.
Then find the product.**

1. $5 \times 9 =$ _____

2. $3 * 6 =$ _____

3. $3 \cdot 9 =$ _____

Ashley drew this large rectangle, which is made up of two small rectangles.

4. Find the area of the large rectangle by finding the areas of the two small rectangles and adding them.

_____

_____

5. Find the area of the large rectangle by multiplying the number of rows by the number of square units in each row.

_____

6. Find this product: $5 \times 6 =$ _____

7. Find this product: $2 \times 6 =$ _____

8. Use your answers to exercises 6 and 7 to find this product: $7 \times 6 =$ _____

Multiplication and Area **179**

Name _____ **Date** _____

Remembering

Use the information in the graph to answer the questions.

1. How many yellow crayons are in the box?

_____

2. How many red and blue crayons are in the box altogether?

_____

3. How many fewer yellow crayons are there than blue crayons?

_____

4. Write a problem using the information in the graph. Solve your problem.

_____

_____

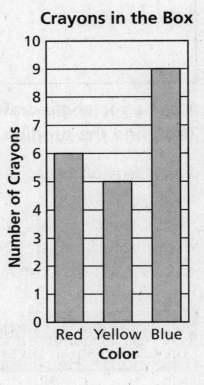

Crayons in the Box

Round each amount to the nearest dime.

5. $5.56 _____ **6.** $6.34 _____ **7.** $4.98 _____ **8.** $7.87 _____

Circle the word that describes each pair of line segments.

9.

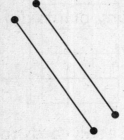

parallel
perpendicular
neither

10.

parallel
perpendicular
neither

11.

parallel
perpendicular
neither

12.

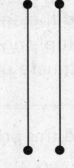

parallel
perpendicular
neither

Multiplication and Area

Study Plan

_____

Homework Helper

Read each problem and decide what type of problem it is from the list. Then write an equation for the problem and solve.

a. Array Multiplication
b. Array Division
c. Repeated-Groups Multiplication
d. Repeated-Groups Division with an Unknown Group Size
e. Repeated-Groups Division with an Unknown Multiplier (number of groups)

1. A farmer collected eggs from the henhouse. He can put 36 eggs in a carton. A carton will hold 6 eggs in a row. How many rows does the egg carton have?

_____

2. The Watertown science contest allowed teams of 5 students to compete. If 45 students entered the contest, how many teams competed?

_____

3. The Happy Feet Shoe Store is having a sale. 10 pairs of shoes are displayed on each row of the sale rack. If the rack has 8 rows, how many pairs of shoes are on sale?

_____

4. Una has 5 goldfish. She bought 2 small water plants for each goldfish. How many plants did she buy?

_____

5. Yolanda made 16 barrettes. She divided the barrettes equally among her 4 friends. How many barrettes did each friend get?

_____

6. Carson has 12 baseball cards to give away. If he gives 3 cards to each friend, how many friends can he give cards to?

_____

Name _____ **Date** _____

Remembering

Solve each problem.

1. Reba had $2.87. She earned $7.62 more. How much money does she have now? _____

2. Toni earned $14.00 babysitting. She spent $3.79 on baseball cards. Then she found $6.50 in her piggy bank. How much money does Toni have now? _____

3. José bought a new bell for his bike for $4.58. Then he bought a new bike helmet for $12.95. How much more did he spend on the helmet than on the bell? _____

Round each number to the nearest ten.

4. 458 _____   5. 792 _____   6. 23 _____

7. 341 _____   8. 127 _____   9. 598 _____

Is the dashed line a line of symmetry for the figure? Write _yes_ or _no_.

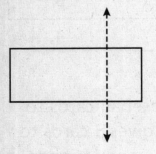

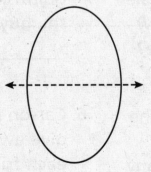

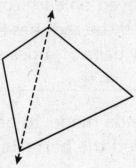

10. _____   11. _____   12. _____

Solve and Create Word Problems

Homework

Use this table to practice your 4s Count-bys, multiplications, and divisions. Then have your homework helper test you.

4s	× In Order	× Mixed Up	÷ Mixed Up
	$1 \times 4 = 4$	$9 \times 4 = 36$	$20 \div 4 = 5$
	$2 \times 4 = 8$	$5 \times 4 = 20$	$4 \div 4 = 1$
	$3 \times 4 = 12$	$7 \times 4 = 28$	$16 \div 4 = 4$
	$4 \times 4 = 16$	$2 \times 4 = 8$	$36 \div 4 = 9$
	$5 \times 4 = 20$	$4 \times 4 = 16$	$24 \div 4 = 6$
	$6 \times 4 = 24$	$1 \times 4 = 4$	$12 \div 4 = 3$
	$7 \times 4 = 28$	$6 \times 4 = 24$	$32 \div 4 = 8$
	$8 \times 4 = 32$	$8 \times 4 = 32$	$8 \div 4 = 2$
	$9 \times 4 = 36$	$3 \times 4 = 12$	$40 \div 4 = 10$
	$10 \times 4 = 40$	$10 \times 4 = 40$	$28 \div 4 = 7$

Homework

Multiply or divide to find the unknown numbers. Then check your answers at the bottom of this page.

1. $4 \times 9 = \boxed{}$ **2.** $12 \div 3 = \boxed{}$ **3.** $4 * 8 = \boxed{}$

4. $30 / 3 = \boxed{}$ **5.** $3 \bullet \boxed{} = 24$ **6.** $9\overline{)81}$

7. $6 \times 3 = \boxed{}$ **8.** $\dfrac{27}{3} = \boxed{}$ **9.** $9 \times 10 = \boxed{}$

10. $24 / 4 = \boxed{}$ **11.** $10 \bullet 3 = \boxed{}$ **12.** $16 \div 4 = \boxed{}$

13. $9 * \boxed{} = 63$ **14.** $\dfrac{36}{4} = \boxed{}$ **15.** $7 \bullet 4 = \boxed{}$

16. $20 / 4 = \boxed{}$ **17.** $9\overline{)54}$ **18.** $3 * 7 = \boxed{}$

19. $\boxed{} \times 4 = 4$ **20.** $15 \div 3 = \boxed{}$ **21.** $4 \times \boxed{} = 16$

1. 36 **2.** 4 **3.** 32 **4.** 10 **5.** 8 **6.** 9 **7.** 18 **8.** 9 **9.** 90 **10.** 6 **11.** 30
12. 4 **13.** 7 **14.** 9 **15.** 28 **16.** 5 **17.** 6 **18.** 21 **19.** 1 **20.** 5 **21.** 4

Multiply and Divide with 4

Homework

Name

Date

Home Check Sheet 4: 3s and 4s

3s Multiplications	3s Divisions	4s Multiplications	4s Divisions
$8 \times 3 = 24$	$9 / 3 = 3$	$1 \times 4 = 4$	$40 / 4 = 10$
$3 \cdot 2 = 6$	$21 \div 3 = 7$	$4 \cdot 5 = 20$	$12 \div 4 = 3$
$3 * 5 = 15$	$27 / 3 = 9$	$8 * 4 = 32$	$24 / 4 = 6$
$10 \times 3 = 30$	$3 \div 3 = 1$	$3 \times 4 = 12$	$8 \div 4 = 2$
$3 \cdot 3 = 9$	$18 / 3 = 6$	$4 \cdot 6 = 24$	$4 / 4 = 1$
$3 * 6 = 18$	$12 \div 3 = 4$	$4 * 9 = 36$	$28 \div 4 = 7$
$7 \times 3 = 21$	$30 / 3 = 10$	$10 \times 4 = 40$	$32 / 4 = 8$
$3 \cdot 9 = 27$	$6 \div 3 = 2$	$4 \cdot 7 = 28$	$16 \div 4 = 4$
$4 * 3 = 12$	$24 / 3 = 8$	$4 * 4 = 16$	$36 / 4 = 9$
$3 \times 1 = 3$	$15 / 3 = 5$	$2 \times 4 = 8$	$20 / 4 = 5$
$3 \cdot 4 = 12$	$21 \div 3 = 7$	$4 \cdot 3 = 12$	$4 \div 4 = 1$
$3 * 3 = 9$	$3 / 3 = 1$	$4 * 2 = 8$	$32 / 4 = 8$
$3 \times 10 = 30$	$9 \div 3 = 3$	$9 \times 4 = 36$	$8 \div 4 = 2$
$2 \cdot 3 = 6$	$27 / 3 = 9$	$1 \cdot 4 = 4$	$16 / 4 = 4$
$3 * 7 = 21$	$30 \div 3 = 10$	$4 * 6 = 24$	$36 \div 4 = 9$
$6 \times 3 = 18$	$18 / 3 = 6$	$5 \times 4 = 20$	$12 / 4 = 3$
$5 \cdot 3 = 15$	$6 \div 3 = 2$	$4 \cdot 4 = 16$	$40 \div 4 = 10$
$3 * 8 = 24$	$15 \div 3 = 5$	$7 * 4 = 28$	$20 / 4 = 5$
$9 \times 3 = 27$	$12 / 3 = 4$	$8 \times 4 = 32$	$24 / 4 = 6$
$2 \cdot 3 = 6$	$24 \div 3 = 8$	$10 \cdot 4 = 40$	$28 \div 4 = 7$

Home Check Sheet 4: 3s and 4s

Name _____ **Date** _____

Homework

Study Plan

_____
Homework Helper

Solve each problem.

1. Colin had 16 puzzles. He gave 4 puzzles to each of his nephews. How many nephews does Colin have?

   _____

2. Allegra listed the names of her classmates in 4 columns, with 7 names in each column. How many classmates does Allegra have?

   _____

This large rectangle is made up of two small rectangles.

3. Find the area of the large rectangle by finding the areas of the two small rectangles and adding them.

   _____

4. Find the area of the large rectangle by multiplying the number of rows by the number of square units in each row.

   _____

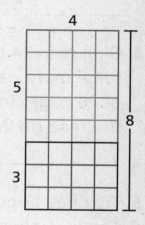

This Equal-Shares drawing shows that 6 groups of 9 is the same as 5 groups of 9 plus 1 group of 9.

5. Find 5 × ⑨ and 1 × ⑨, and add the answers.

   _____

6. Find 6 × ⑨. Did you get the same answer as in question 5?

   _____

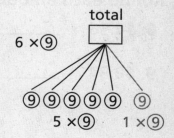

Remembering

Solve each word problem. Label your answer.

> Lewis had 542 seashells. His sister gave him her collection of 231 seashells.

1. How many seashells does Lewis have now?

_____

2. Write a subtraction word problem related to the addition word problem.

_____

_____

3. Without doing any calculations, find the solution to the problem you wrote.

_____

4. Gina read 14 pages of her book on Tuesday and some more pages on Wednesday. She read a total of 26 pages in those two days. How many pages did she read on Wednesday?

_____

5. Troy has 17 goldfish. He has 8 more goldfish than Tomas. How many goldfish does Tomas have?

_____

Round each amount to the nearest dollar.

6. $4.56 _____   **7.** $5.67 _____   **8.** $3.21 _____

9. $8.34 _____   **10.** $4.17 _____   **11.** $9.85 _____

Multiply and Divide with 4

Study Plan

_____

Homework Helper

Solve.

1. Pablo hung his watercolor paintings in an array with 3 rows and 4 columns. How many paintings did Pablo hang?

   _____

2. A group of 7 friends went on a hiking trip. Each person took 3 granola bars. What total number of granola bars did the friends take?

   _____

3. Jon had 45 sheets of construction paper. He used 9 sheets to make paper snowflakes. How many sheets does he have now?

   _____

You can combine multiplications you know to find multiplications you don't know.

4. Find this product: $5 \times 8 =$ _____

5. Find this product: $1 \times 8 =$ _____

6. Use the answers to numbers 4 and 5 to find this product: $6 \times 8 =$ _____

Name _____   **Date** _____

Remembering

Use mental math to subtract.

1. $130 - 60 =$ _____   **2.** $1,100 - 700 =$ _____   **3.** $150 - 90 =$ _____

4. $1,600 - 800 =$ _____   **5.** $120 - 80 =$ _____   **6.** $1,300 - 400 =$ _____

Write a multiplication equation to represent the area of each rectangle.

7.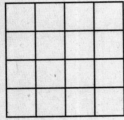

_____

8.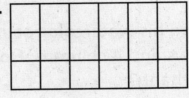

_____

9.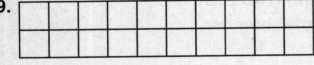

_____

10.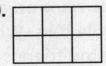

_____

Solve.

11. Mai went to the movies 9 times this month.
She paid 4 dollars to see each movie. How
much did she spend at the movies?

_____

12. Tess had 45 tomato seeds to plant in her
garden. She planted them in an array with
9 rows. How many seeds were in each row?

_____

Use the Strategy Cards

	× In Order	× Mixed Up	÷ Mixed Up
1s	$1 \times 1 = 1$	$3 \times 1 = 3$	$7 \div 1 = 7$
	$2 \times 1 = 2$	$7 \times 1 = 7$	$10 \div 1 = 10$
	$3 \times 1 = 3$	$1 \times 1 = 1$	$3 \div 1 = 3$
	$4 \times 1 = 4$	$10 \times 1 = 10$	$9 \div 1 = 9$
	$5 \times 1 = 5$	$6 \times 1 = 6$	$1 \div 1 = 1$
	$6 \times 1 = 6$	$2 \times 1 = 2$	$4 \div 1 = 4$
	$7 \times 1 = 7$	$5 \times 1 = 5$	$5 \div 1 = 5$
	$8 \times 1 = 8$	$8 \times 1 = 8$	$8 \div 1 = 8$
	$9 \times 1 = 9$	$4 \times 1 = 4$	$2 \div 1 = 2$
	$10 \times 1 = 10$	$9 \times 1 = 9$	$6 \div 1 = 6$

	× In Order	× Mixed Up
0s	$1 \times 0 = 0$	$3 \times 0 = 0$
	$2 \times 0 = 0$	$7 \times 0 = 0$
	$3 \times 0 = 0$	$1 \times 0 = 0$
	$4 \times 0 = 0$	$10 \times 0 = 0$
	$5 \times 0 = 0$	$6 \times 0 = 0$
	$6 \times 0 = 0$	$2 \times 0 = 0$
	$7 \times 0 = 0$	$5 \times 0 = 0$
	$8 \times 0 = 0$	$8 \times 0 = 0$
	$9 \times 0 = 0$	$4 \times 0 = 0$
	$10 \times 0 = 0$	$9 \times 0 = 0$

Name _____ **Date** _____

Homework

**Find the unknown numbers. Then check your answers
at the bottom of this page.**

1. $4 \times 1 = \boxed{}$

2. $12 \div 3 = \boxed{}$

3. $7 * 0 = \boxed{}$

4. $0 / 5 = \boxed{}$

5. $4 \bullet \boxed{} = 8$

6. $\dfrac{2}{1} = \boxed{}$

7. $10 \times 1 = \boxed{}$

8. $\dfrac{0}{4} = \boxed{}$

9. $1 \times 0 = \boxed{}$

10. $3\overline{)9}$ with box above

11. $10 \bullet 9 = \boxed{}$

12. $0 \div 1 = \boxed{}$

13. $3 * \boxed{} = 3$

14. $\dfrac{8}{1} = \boxed{}$

15. $0 \bullet 7 = \boxed{}$

16. $24 / 3 = \boxed{}$

17. $1 \div 1 = \boxed{}$

18. $10 * 2 = \boxed{}$

19. $\boxed{} \times 3 = 0$

20. $3\overline{)18}$ with box above

21. $1 \times \boxed{} = 4$

22. $\boxed{} \times 5 = 25$

23. $6 \bullet 9 = \boxed{}$

24. $10 \div 1 = \boxed{}$

23. 54 **24.** 10
13. 1 **14.** 8 **15.** 0 **16.** 8 **17.** 1 **18.** 20 **19.** 0 **20.** 6 **21.** 4 **22.** 5
1. 4 **2.** 4 **3.** 0 **4.** 0 **5.** 2 **6.** 2 **7.** 10 **8.** 0 **9.** 0 **10.** 3 **11.** 90 **12.** 0

Multiply and Divide with 1 and 0

Homework

┌───┐
│ **Study Plan**   │
│   │
│   │
│   _____   │
│   Homework Helper   │
└───┘

Complete.

1. $3 \times (4 \times 2) = \square$ **2.** $(5 \times 2) \times 8 = \square$ **3.** $5 \times (0 \times 9) = \square$

4. $25 \times 1 = \square$ **5.** $3 \times 9 = 9 \times \square = \square$ **6.** $6 \times (3 \times 2) = \square$

Solve each problem.

7. Paul put birthday candles on his brother's cake. He arranged them in an array with 8 rows and 1 column. How many candles did he put on the cake? _____

8. There are 24 people in the brass section of the marching band. They stood in an array with 4 people in each row. How many rows were there? _____

9. Freya doesn't like peppers, so she grew 0 peppers in her garden. She divided the peppers equally among her 4 cousins. How many peppers did each cousin get? _____

10. Cal had 6 comic books. After he gave 1 comic book to each of his cousins, he had none left. How many cousins does Cal have? _____

Name _____   **Date** _____

Remembering

Solve each problem.   *Show your work.*

1. Dakota had some money. Then she earned $6.84 at her family's garage sale. Now she has $9.75. How much money did she start with?

   _____

2. Frankie's dog weighs 82 pounds. His cat weighs 17 pounds. How much less does his cat weigh than his dog?

   _____

3. Ghita had 9 trophies. 4 were tennis trophies, and the rest were soccer trophies. Then she won 3 more soccer trophies. How many soccer trophies does Ghita have now?

   _____

Draw three different coin combinations for each amount.

4. 73¢	5. $0.32	6. 57¢
_____	_____	_____
_____	_____	_____
_____	_____	_____

Add or subtract.

7. $500 - 327 =$ _____   8. $87 + 264 =$ _____   9. $902 - 209 =$ _____

Multiply and Divide with 1 and 0

Home Check Sheet 5: 1s and 0s

1s Multiplications	1s Divisions	0s Multiplications
1 × 4 = 4	10 / 1 = 10	4 × 0 = 0
5 • 1 = 5	5 ÷ 1 = 5	2 • 0 = 0
7 * 1 = 7	7 / 1 = 7	0 * 8 = 0
1 × 8 = 8	9 ÷ 1 = 9	0 × 5 = 0
1 • 6 = 6	3 / 1 = 3	6 • 0 = 0
10 * 1 = 10	10 ÷ 1 = 10	0 * 7 = 0
1 × 9 = 9	2 / 1 = 2	0 × 2 = 0
3 • 1 = 3	8 ÷ 1 = 8	0 • 9 = 0
1 * 2 = 2	6 / 1 = 6	10 * 0 = 0
1 × 1 = 1	9 / 1 = 9	1 × 0 = 0
8 • 1 = 8	1 ÷ 1 = 1	0 • 6 = 0
1 * 7 = 7	5 / 1 = 5	9 * 0 = 0
1 × 5 = 5	3 ÷ 1 = 3	0 × 4 = 0
6 • 1 = 6	4 / 1 = 4	3 • 0 = 0
1 * 1 = 1	2 ÷ 1 = 2	0 * 3 = 0
1 × 10 = 10	8 / 1 = 8	8 × 0 = 0
9 • 1 = 9	4 ÷ 1 = 4	0 • 10 = 0
4 * 1 = 4	7 ÷ 1 = 7	0 * 1 = 0
2 × 1 = 2	1 / 1 = 1	5 × 0 = 0
1 • 3 = 3	6 ÷ 1 = 6	7 • 0 = 0

Home Check Sheet 6: Mixed 3s, 4s, 0s, and 1s

3s, 4s, 0s, 1s Multiplications	3s, 4s, 0s, 1s Multiplications	3s, 4s, 1s Divisions	3s, 4s, 1s Divisions
$5 \times 3 = 15$	$0 \times 5 = 0$	$18 / 3 = 6$	$4 / 1 = 4$
$6 \cdot 4 = 24$	$10 \cdot 1 = 10$	$20 \div 4 = 5$	$21 \div 3 = 7$
$9 * 0 = 0$	$6 * 3 = 18$	$1 / 1 = 1$	$16 / 4 = 4$
$7 \times 1 = 7$	$2 \times 4 = 8$	$21 \div 3 = 7$	$9 \div 1 = 9$
$3 \cdot 3 = 9$	$5 \cdot 0 = 0$	$12 / 4 = 3$	$15 / 3 = 5$
$4 * 7 = 28$	$1 * 2 = 2$	$5 \div 1 = 5$	$8 \div 4 = 2$
$0 \times 10 = 0$	$10 \times 3 = 30$	$15 / 3 = 5$	$5 / 1 = 5$
$1 \cdot 6 = 6$	$5 \cdot 4 = 20$	$24 \div 4 = 6$	$30 \div 3 = 10$
$3 * 4 = 12$	$0 * 8 = 0$	$7 / 1 = 7$	$12 / 4 = 3$
$5 \times 4 = 20$	$9 \times 2 = 18$	$12 / 3 = 4$	$8 / 1 = 8$
$0 \cdot 5 = 0$	$10 \cdot 3 = 30$	$36 \div 4 = 9$	$27 \div 3 = 9$
$9 * 1 = 9$	$9 * 4 = 36$	$6 / 1 = 6$	$40 / 4 = 10$
$2 \times 3 = 6$	$1 \times 0 = 0$	$12 \div 3 = 4$	$4 \div 1 = 4$
$3 \cdot 4 = 12$	$1 \cdot 6 = 6$	$16 / 4 = 4$	$9 / 3 = 3$
$0 * 9 = 0$	$3 * 6 = 18$	$7 \div 1 = 7$	$16 \div 4 = 4$
$1 \times 5 = 5$	$7 \times 4 = 28$	$9 / 3 = 3$	$10 / 1 = 10$
$2 \cdot 3 = 6$	$6 \cdot 0 = 0$	$8 \div 4 = 2$	$9 \div 3 = 3$
$4 * 4 = 16$	$8 * 1 = 8$	$2 \div 1 = 2$	$20 \div 4 = 5$
$9 \times 0 = 0$	$3 \times 9 = 27$	$6 / 3 = 2$	$6 / 1 = 6$
$1 \cdot 1 = 1$	$1 \cdot 4 = 4$	$32 \div 4 = 8$	$24 \div 3 = 8$

Homework

Study Plan

Homework Helper

Solve each problem.

Show your work.

1. Wendy gave 54 apples to her neighbors. She gave away a total of 6 bags of apples. How many apples were in each bag?

   _____

2. Dillon had a box of 45 toy trucks. He gave the trucks to his brother but kept 9 trucks for himself. How many trucks did Dillon give to his brother?

   _____

3. Melissa put 18 stickers in her new sticker album. She put them in 6 rows. How many stickers did she put in each row?

   _____

4. Yan took photographs at the zoo. He took 5 photos in each of the 6 animal houses. How many photos did he take?

   _____

5. Janie stacked some books at the library. She stacked 8 books in 7 different piles. How many books were in the piles?

   _____

Remembering

Use mental math to find the answer.

1. 40 + 80 − 20 = ____ **2.** 150 − 70 + 30 = ____ **3.** 80 + 80 − 30 = ____

4. 70 + 40 − 50 = ____ **5.** 130 − 50 + 70 = ____ **6.** 170 − 90 − 30 = ____

Solve each problem.

7. Ants have 6 legs. How many legs are on 8 ants? Find the total by starting with the fifth count-by and counting up from there.

_____

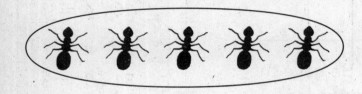

____ ____ ____ ____

8. How many roses are in these 6 vases? Find the total by starting with the fifth count-by and counting up from there.

_____

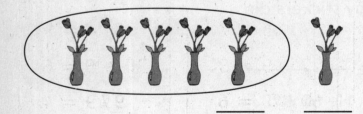

____ ____

This Equal-Shares Drawing shows that 6 groups of 4 is the same as 4 groups of 4 plus 2 groups of 4.

9. Find 4 × ④ and 2 × ④ and add the answers.

_____

10. Find 6 × ④. Did you get the same answer as in number 9?

_____

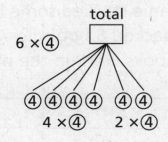

Home Check Sheet 7: 0s, 1s, 2s, 3s, 4s, 5s, 9s, and 10s

0s, 1s, 2s, 3s, 4s, 5s, 9s, 10s Multiplications	0s, 1s, 2s, 3s, 4s, 5s, 9s, 10s Multiplications	1s, 2s, 3s, 4s, 5s, 9s, 10s Divisions	1s, 2s, 3s, 4s, 5s, 9s, 10s Divisions
$3 \times 0 = 0$	$0 \times 4 = 0$	$9 / 1 = 9$	$40 / 10 = 4$
$7 \cdot 1 = 7$	$5 \cdot 1 = 5$	$4 \div 2 = 2$	$7 \div 1 = 7$
$2 * 2 = 4$	$6 * 7 = 42$	$9 / 3 = 3$	$16 / 2 = 8$
$1 \times 3 = 3$	$2 \times 3 = 6$	$20 \div 4 = 5$	$18 \div 3 = 6$
$4 \cdot 4 = 16$	$5 \cdot 0 = 0$	$15 / 5 = 3$	$16 / 4 = 4$
$6 * 5 = 30$	$1 * 1 = 1$	$45 \div 9 = 5$	$50 \div 5 = 10$
$5 \times 9 = 45$	$10 \times 2 = 20$	$50 / 10 = 5$	$81 / 9 = 9$
$0 \cdot 10 = 0$	$5 \cdot 3 = 15$	$10 \div 1 = 10$	$30 \div 10 = 3$
$0 * 4 = 0$	$4 * 5 = 20$	$8 / 2 = 4$	$10 / 1 = 10$
$1 \times 8 = 8$	$5 \times 6 = 30$	$12 / 3 = 4$	$8 / 2 = 4$
$2 \cdot 5 = 10$	$9 \cdot 7 = 63$	$16 \div 4 = 4$	$27 \div 3 = 9$
$3 * 2 = 6$	$4 * 10 = 40$	$35 / 5 = 7$	$36 / 4 = 9$
$4 \times 3 = 12$	$6 \times 0 = 0$	$27 \div 9 = 3$	$30 \div 5 = 6$
$5 \cdot 4 = 20$	$1 \cdot 6 = 6$	$60 / 10 = 6$	$9 / 9 = 1$
$9 * 6 = 54$	$3 * 2 = 6$	$7 \div 1 = 7$	$80 \div 10 = 8$
$10 \times 7 = 70$	$7 \times 3 = 21$	$8 / 2 = 4$	$10 / 1 = 10$
$0 \cdot 8 = 0$	$4 \cdot 0 = 0$	$18 \div 3 = 6$	$4 \div 2 = 2$
$4 * 9 = 36$	$9 * 5 = 40$	$12 \div 4 = 3$	$21 \div 3 = 7$
$2 \times 0 = 0$	$4 \times 9 = 36$	$40 / 5 = 8$	$8 / 4 = 2$
$1 \cdot 3 = 3$	$10 \cdot 5 = 50$	$36 \div 9 = 4$	$25 \div 5 = 5$

Name _____ **Date** _____

Homework

Find the unknown numbers. Then check your answers at the bottom of this page.

1. $6 \times 3 = \boxed{}$

2. $8 \div 2 = \boxed{}$

3. $5 * 0 = \boxed{}$

4. $4 / 2 = \boxed{}$

5. $3 \bullet \boxed{} = 6$

6. $\dfrac{7}{1} = \boxed{}$

7. $9 \times 1 = \boxed{}$

8. $\dfrac{0}{5} = \boxed{}$

9. $1 \times 6 = \boxed{}$

10. $4\overline{)8}$ with $\boxed{}$ above

11. $6 \bullet 4 = \boxed{}$

12. $0 \div 4 = \boxed{}$

13. $5 * \boxed{} = 10$

14. $\dfrac{9}{1} = \boxed{}$

15. $0 \bullet 1 = \boxed{}$

16. $\dfrac{25}{5} = \boxed{}$

17. $2 \div 2 = \boxed{}$

18. $8 * 2 = \boxed{}$

19. $\boxed{} \times 7 = 0$

20. $3\overline{)18}$ with $\boxed{}$ above

21. $1 * \boxed{} = 8$

22. $\boxed{} \times 3 = 9$

23. $4 \bullet 9 = \boxed{}$

24. $3 \div 1 = \boxed{}$

1. 18 **2.** 4 **3.** 0 **4.** 2 **5.** 2 **6.** 7 **7.** 9 **8.** 0 **9.** 6 **10.** 2
11. 24 **12.** 0 **13.** 2 **14.** 9 **15.** 0 **16.** 5 **17.** 1 **18.** 16 **19.** 0
20. 6 **21.** 8 **22.** 3 **23.** 36 **24.** 3

Practice with 0s, 1s, 2s, 3s, 4s, 5s, 9s, and 10s

Name

Date

Study Plan

_____

Homework Helper

Solve each problem.

1. Maili rode her bike 10 miles every day for 5 days. How many miles did she ride?

   _____

2. Leslie gave 72 balloons to children at the fair. After the fair, she had 9 balloons left. How many balloons did Leslie start with?

   _____

3. Tony hung some photographs on one wall in his room. He hung them in 3 rows, with 4 photos in each row. How many photos did Tony hang?

   _____

4. Pepe sent 15 gifts to his family members. He sent an equal amount of gifts to 3 different addresses. How many gifts did he send to each address?

   _____

5. At the Shady Acres Stables, there are 5 horses in each barn. There are 4 barns. How many horses are at Shady Acres?

   _____

6. Sixty students are in the marching band. There are 10 rows. How many students are in each row?

   _____

7. Danielle has 35 dolls in her collection. She wants to display them on 5 shelves. How many dolls should she put on each shelf?

   _____

8. There are 9 players on a baseball team. There are 6 teams in the league. How many baseball players are in the league?

   _____

Remembering

Solve each problem.

1. How many ears are on 6 dogs? Find the total by starting with the fifth count-by and counting up from there.

   _____

   _____   _____

2. How many pancakes are in these 7 stacks? Find the total by starting with the fifth count-by and counting up from there.

   _____

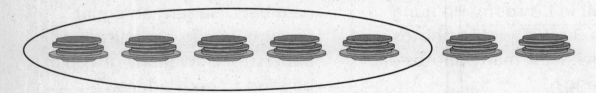

   _____   _____   _____

Complete.

3. Find the area of the large rectangle by finding the areas of the two small rectangles and adding them.

   _____

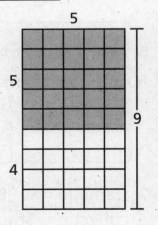

4. Find the area of the large rectangle by multiplying the number of rows by the number of square units in each row.

   _____

5. Find this product: $3 \times 6 =$ _____

6. Find this product: $4 \times 6 =$ _____

7. Use your answers to exercises 5 and 6 to find this product: $7 \times 6 =$ _____

Practice with 0s, 1s, 2s, 3s, 4s, 5s, 9s, and 10s

Name _____   **Date** _____

Homework

Connections

Write two word problems about your family or friends. Give the answer to the problem.

_____

_____

_____

_____

_____

_____

_____

_____

Reasoning and Proof

Rama is going to buy 2 charms. The dog charm costs 23¢, the cat charm cost 30¢, the bird charm costs 25¢, and the fish charm costs 20¢. What are all the possible amounts of money Rama might spend? How do you know you found all the possibilities?

_____

_____

_____

_____

_____

_____

_____

Communication

77 + 31 + 28

What is a good estimate for the answer to the problem above? How did you estimate?

_____

_____

_____

Representation

Here is a pattern.

A B B A B B A B B

Make the same kind of pattern with shapes.

Name _____

Date _____

Remembering

Draw the hands on the clock to show the time.

1.

| 2:30 | 9:15 | 3:00 |

Write the time on the digital clock.

2.

  [ ]

Complete the number sequence. Write the rule.

3. 10, 17, 24, _____, _____, _____   Rule: _____

4. 53, 55, 57, _____, _____, _____   Rule: _____

5. 68, 64, 60, _____, _____, _____   Rule: _____

Use Mathematical Processes